TC STUDIES
IN EDUCATION

RECENT TITLES

FACULTY RIGHTS

AND OBLIGATIONS

IN EIGHT INDEPENDENT

LIBERAL ARTS COLLEGES

BY CHARLES P. DENNISON

ASSISTANT TO THE DEAN OF THE GRADUATE
SCHOOL, PRINCETON UNIVERSITY

BUREAU OF PUBLICATIONS

TEACHERS COLLEGE, COLUMBIA, 1955

MANUFACTURED IN THE UNITED STATES OF AMERICA

ACKNOWLEDGMENTS

The facts, interpretations, and ideas that have been brought together in this book represent many sources, and the book would not be complete without mention of the extent of the writer's debt to the people whose aid it embodies in one way or another. Their contributions range from factual information to interpretations based on long personal experience with the matters under study. In less direct ways, the counsel of many people has affected the study through its impact on the writer's thinking.

Foremost is his debt to his major adviser, Professor Karl W. Bigelow, of Teachers College, Columbia University, whose critical guidance, encouragement, and assistance throughout were most generous; and to the other members of the doctoral committee, Professor John L. Childs and Professor Thad L. Hungate, whose incisive and well-timed questions helped to keep the writer's efforts in channels relevant to the purposes of the study, and whose confidence in the outcome provided continuing support through difficult phases of the work. The writer's special thanks go also to Dr. Ronald C. Bauer, who, although not a member of the committee, responded most helpfully to the need for counsel on numerous occasions.

Since the study required the availability of much source material and many conferences with staff members of the eight colleges concerned, the writer is indebted for the necessary co-operation to President Sarah Gibson Blanding of Vassar College, President Alan Willard Brown of the Colleges of the Seneca, President Victor Lloyd Butterfield of Wesleyan University, President Everett N. Case of Colgate University, President Roswell Gray Ham of Mount Holyoke College, former President John W. Nason of Swarthmore College, President Harold Taylor of Sarah Lawrence College, and President Gilbert Fowler White of Haverford College.

Thanks are due for innumerable contributions of information and ideas by the other administrative officers and teaching faculty members with whom the writer had the privilege of conferring, whose diverse views contributed greatly to his thinking, and many of whose statements are directly reported in the text. Particular thanks are due to members of elected faculty advisory bodies in several of the colleges for their painstaking checking of the writer's version of principles and practices.

Others whose counsel has been greatly appreciated are Henry Noble MacCracken, president emeritus of Vassar College; Ewald B. Nyquist, assistant commissioner for higher education, New York State Department of Education; and Professor Paul W. Ward of Syracuse University, chairman of Committee T of the American Association of University Professors.

The writer assumes full responsibility for the use he has made of all the help hereby acknowledged, and for all statements, interpretations, and conclusions not specifically attributed to others.

C. P. D.

PREFACE

The study on which this book is based was made to determine how the formal expression of faculty members' rights and obligations, in more or less constitutional statements and procedures, might contribute to their realization and to the development of sound relationships within an institution. The specific questions to which answers were sought in each of the eight colleges studied were (1) what the formal provisions relating to faculty rights and obligations actually were; (2) how such provisions came to be adopted; (3) how they operated in practice; (4) what the principal opinions regarding them were; and (5) what tendencies, if any, were indicated for the future.

To permit the type of inquiry that promised to yield the maximum usable data for the time and energy spent, the selection of institutions was made with particular attention to the following: (1) accessibility for campus visits from New York; (2) sufficient homogeneity in type, purpose, and size to assure some basis for comparison of experience; and (3) sufficient variation within basic points of resemblance to assure a variety of experience for analysis.

The group selected consisted of eight independent[1] liberal arts

[1] The term *independent* as used in this study refers to the legal status of the corporation of an institution. It means that appointments to the governing board

colleges with enrollments of less than fifteen hundred students
and with fewer than three graduate divisions. Three of the colleges are for men only; three are for women only; one is coeducational; and one is the men's unit of a dual structure.[2] Three
of the colleges have Protestant connections, though these are connections of association and not of control.

Data for the study were obtained in part from college documents and in part from guided interviews with instructional and
administrative officers. Interviews were based on a clear organization of the topic but did not have an obligatory schedule of questions. The purpose of this approach was to assist the people
interviewed to search for whatever, out of their experience,
seemed most relevant to the topic. The material gathered in the
interviews ranged, of course, from isolated observations to comprehensive interpretations.

The topical framework for the study was the postulated Academic Bill of Rights and Obligations, which is discussed in
Chapter I. Induced from the formal documents of these and
other colleges, this framework was modified from time to time to
accommodate principles and practices first encountered in the
eight institutions studied. At each college, specific questions
based on preliminary comparison of the documents of that institution with those of others were raised.

The persons whom the writer sought to interview were, in
general, those who had had most experience with the formulation of by-laws and other prescriptive documents, those who were
otherwise involved in matters related to the topic, and some of

---

are, in general, free from control by either public or sectarian authority. In this
sense, although three of the colleges have religious connections, they are nevertheless independent. The corporation of the Colleges of the Seneca has one ex
officio trustee who is an official of a religious denomination. Most Swarthmore
board members are, and all Haverford board members are required to be, Quakers,
but these members are elected as individuals and are not responsible to the religious
body in the discharge of their responsibilities.

[2] Much of the descriptive material given throughout this book about Hobart
College really pertains to the dual collegiate organization, Colleges of the Seneca,
of which Hobart and William Smith Colleges, for men and women respectively,
are the component units. The same corporate documents apply to both colleges,
and there is one faculty for the two units. The writer did not, however, interview administrative officers serving only William Smith College.

those who might have an important view to present on some limited aspect of it—for example, junior officers of instruction without continuous tenure. The conferences, which usually lasted from a half hour to an hour, were sometimes arranged through the president's office, at the writer's request, and sometimes by the writer himself, who was usually invited to see whomever he wished. Persons interviewed at each college included administrative officers and teaching faculty members of varying seniority.

Additional historical materials, while not examined systematically or thoroughly, were occasionally used to supplement the data gathered from current documents of government and from personal interviews. Both factual information and interpretations were checked on subsequent visits to each campus.

The task of this study included both the gathering and systematizing of information and its critical interpretation. Chapter II contains a summary and comparison of the provisions found in each of the eight colleges for the application of the principles embodied in the postulated Academic Bill of Rights and Obligations. The raw data on which this chapter is based have been edited and organized in outline form in the Comparative Synopsis (see pp. 124–179). Chapter III is devoted to a consideration of the experience of four of the institutions in the area of faculty rights and obligations. Chapter IV contains the writer's main synthesizing efforts and conclusions. His own conclusions go somewhat beyond those that logically follow from the evidence presented throughout the book and are, therefore, presented separately.

It is an act of interpretation to select from the subjectively reported experience of a college and from its current statutes and other documents the facts pertinent to a description of its formalization of faculty rights and obligations. A complete coverage of pertinent facts, moreover, is presumably impossible. Hence, although the writer has tried to support every inference with facts, there may be room for legitimate dissent. He has done his best, however, to indicate the extent of fact, of reported fact, and of inference, and to give effect to these distinctions in the tentativeness or finality with which resulting interpretations are stated.

The factual data on which the report is based, many of which are presented in the Comparative Synopsis, were collected largely during or prior to March, 1953. Since revisions of formally stated rights and obligations were then in progress in several of the colleges, some of the material presented here will already be out of date. The writer was able, however, through the assistance of officers in these institutions, to report certain significant changes in progress at that time, thus bringing the record of conditions up to date through the academic year 1952–53.

C. P. D.

Princeton, New Jersey
August, 1954

CONTENTS

FACULTY RIGHTS

AND OBLIGATIONS

IN EIGHT INDEPENDENT

LIBERAL ARTS COLLEGES

AN ACADEMIC BILL

OF RIGHTS

AND OBLIGATIONS

THE NEED FOR CLARIFICATION

It is widely agreed that the college faculty member has a particular role to play in our society, as teachers and scholars have a distinctive part in other societies. The precise definition of that role in the United States, however, has long been controversial, and the scholar's function as he understands it may be very different from that which is assigned to him by various other groups to which he must relate himself. Indeed, it has not been generally agreed on even within the academic profession just what the rights and obligations of the scholar-teacher are.

Although this book does not pretend to settle the persistent and highly complex question of the faculty member's role, it does postulate, and to some extent evaluate, a coherent body of principles and related practices based on what certain institutions have formulated and carried out. The examination and interpretation of the experience of a group of colleges in the area of faculty rights and obligations will, it is hoped, be of use to a profession that must concern itself with the clarification of its functions and the responsibilities of its members in the performance of these functions. If the teacher's prerogatives and responsibilities were clearer to the profession itself, they would tend also to be clearer to the people at large. In the presence of such improved rapport, politically inspired public investigations, which thrive on group misunderstandings, would lose that devastating impact which has been felt by the educational world during the past several years.

VIEWS RELATING TO THE FACULTY MEMBER'S ROLE

Older issues: The employee concept vs. the partnership concept

An issue that has been central throughout much of the development of American higher education arises from the place of learning in the culture and, hence, from the prestige of the man of learning in society. (Shryock,[1] for example, found a striking discrepancy between the general regard for scholars in Germany and in the United States.) This issue has often been identified, with considerable accuracy, as that of whether the faculty member is primarily an employee of a corporation, which legally he is, or whether he is a full-fledged partner in a cooperative enterprise that, for practical reasons, has been organized as a corporation. Presumably, no reputable educator would view a faculty member merely as a special type of corporation employee; nevertheless, some of those who believe strongly in the operating control of institutions by their faculties do not deny that the governing board should have the final legal authority, even though they are opposed to the arbitrary use of such authority.

The following two passages exemplify this contrast in attitude, which has such profound significance for the role of the individual faculty member. The author of the first quotation regards the

[1] R. H. Shryock, "The Academic Profession in the United States," AAUP *Bulletin*, 38:32, Spring 1952.

teacher as a hired person whose initiative must be subordinate to his employer's purposes:

Every great industrial institution and most of the professional organizations has [sic] a policy, a well-defined policy that it follows. I don't see any reason why it is not the function of a university board of trustees to have a well-defined policy that should be followed in the institution which it is seeking to govern. If that policy [were] followed consistently by board after board, you would finally have your faculty dropping into that policy and giving your institution a reputation that would draw to you a great class of noble men and women for education. I believe we fail in not having well-defined policies particular to our institutions.

Let me illustrate that by an example. In these institutions there is a term *Academic Freedom* . . . .

I do not believe any state institution can for a single minute permit a member of the faculty to serve upon its payroll and to teach the expanding minds of the young people of the coming generation that the Constitution of the United States is a worn-out document.[2]

The second passage states the opposing position:

. . . I have always refused to consider myself in the light of an employee of the president and board, but rather as a co-worker in a mutual administration of a trust in which they have their part and I have mine—and this despite the fact that they have the undoubted legal power to "dismiss" me and I have not that to dismiss them, this being merely one of the differentiations of functions in the administration of the trust.[3]

Studies by the American Association of University Professors.— The issue identified in the preceding paragraphs has been the source of repeated conflict since the last century, and considerable organized study has been given to it, particularly since the founding of the American Association of University Professors in 1915. Out of the activities of the Association have come not only investigations of particular institutional situations but also general studies and statements of principles, including the 1940

[2] D. L. Gaskill, "The Functions of Governing Boards," Association of Governing Boards of State Universities and Allied Institutions, *Proceedings* (Chicago: The Association, 1924), p. 44.

[3] Statement of a Stanford University professor, as quoted in U. Sinclair, *The Goose-Step: A Study of American Education*, 1923, p. 456.

3

"Statement of Principles on Academic Freedom and Tenure" and its predecessor statements of 1915 and 1925. The 1940 statement, formulated by the Association's Committee on Academic Freedom and Tenure (Committee A) and endorsed both by the Association and by the Association of American Colleges, is too well known to require quoting here.[4] It is referred to throughout this report as the AAUP–AAC *Principles*.

The other committee of the American Association of University Professors whose work is of great importance to this study is Committee T, the Committee on the Place and Function of Faculties in College and University Government.[5] Committee T began its work in 1917 with an examination of the effective status of faculties in relation to those matters of university government and administration in which it was believed the faculty should have a part. The questions concerned specific practices with respect to (1) faculty representation on the governing board and (2) faculty participation in such areas as selection of the chief executive of the institution; selection of the other administrative officers; determination of faculty appointments, promotions, and separations; setting of over-all policies of the institution; and planning of the educational program. The Committee's conclusion,[6] published in 1920, was that the extent of democratic participation of faculties in university government and administration was negligible compared to what it should be.

Ten years after the first study by Committee T, Ashbrook,[7]

[4] The 1915 "Declaration of Principles" was prepared and endorsed by the American Association of University Professors. The 1925 "Conference Statement on Academic Freedom and Tenure" was endorsed by the Association of American Colleges in 1925 and by the American Association of University Professors in 1926. The 1940 statement was endorsed, in 1941, not only by these two organizations but also by the American Association of Teachers Colleges, whose successor, the American Association of Colleges for Teacher Education, endorsed it in 1950. Since 1941 it has been further endorsed by several other educational associations.

[5] The exact designation of Committee T's assignment has varied slightly over the years. The titles of some of its reports omit the words "College and"; and sometimes the words "Government and Administration" are used rather than the single word "Government."

[6] "Report of Committee T on the Place and Function of Faculties in University Government and Administration," J. A. Leighton, Chairman, AAUP *Bulletin*, 6:17–47, March 1920.

[7] W. A. Ashbrook, "The Organization and Activities of Boards Which Control Institutions of Higher Learning," 1930.

using the same questions, conducted a follow-up survey of the same institutions that had been included in the 1920 study, with the aim of discovering trends in the democratization of the role of faculties. He found that no democratizing changes of great consequence had taken place in the ten-year interval between the two studies, some liberalization being apparent in certain areas while a slight regression toward more authoritarian practices had appeared in others. His conclusion was, however, that a "slow liberalization" had been taking place.

Committee T has conducted further studies of college and university government, which have been reported in the AAUP *Bulletin* from time to time.[8] Perhaps the most significant document, for its bearing on the present study, is the 1937 statement of the Committee's philosophy of the government of higher education. This statement, as it appears in the Committee's report of 1948, is quoted below:

I. There ought to be close understanding between the faculty and the board of trustees, and to this end agencies other than the president are required for joint conference between the two bodies.

II. The general faculty should participate with the trustees in the nomination of a president, and the faculty of a school or division should have a voice in selecting the dean who presides over that school.

III. Administrative officers should have the advice of representative faculty committees in matters of educational policy, and specifically in matters touching appointments, promotions and dismissals, and in making budgets.

IV. The faculty of the university at large or its authorized representatives, and the faculty of each college in the university, should have ultimate legislative power over educational policies within the jurisdiction of that faculty, and should control its own organization and its committees.

V. The departments of instruction, however organized, should be consultative bodies and should exercise what is in effect a collective authority over the teaching and research under their jurisdiction.[9]

[8] Studies prior to 1948 are described in Committee T's report for that year. See "The Role of Faculties in College and University Government," P. W. Ward, Chairman, AAUP *Bulletin*, 34:55–66, Spring 1948. The study currently in progress is described in "The Place and Function of Faculties in College and University Government; Report of Progress," P. W. Ward, Chairman, AAUP *Bulletin*, 39:300–318, Summer 1953.

[9] "The Role of Faculties in College and University Government," P. W. Ward, Chairman, AAUP *Bulletin*, 38:58–59, Spring 1948.

Views expressed by individual writers.—During the period covered by the work of Committee A and Committee T, a number of individual writers, often aroused by violations of what they considered faculty members' individual rights, expressed themselves forcefully on the subject of university government. Much bitter criticism of the American system of college and university control has indeed been written, and extreme solutions, such as that of abolishing lay governing boards and establishing a type of control similar to that prevailing in the two oldest English universities, have occasionally been proposed. The severest critics attributed many, if not most, of the evils in higher educational administration to the control of colleges and universities by men of narrow or selfish purpose, men strong in economic power and weak in intellectual and spiritual values.

The several scholars who have written vigorously concerning the abuses of the system of college and university government in the United States have differed with one another both in their evaluation of the seriousness of the situation and in their proposed solutions. The more extreme view is that lay governing boards, in their existing form, should be abolished. Kirkpatrick and Sinclair,[10] for example, have taken this position. Among the less extreme measures that have been, and continue to be, urged are changes in the composition of governing boards. At least three recent proposals[11] favored faculty representation as a general practice.

A number of more moderate voices in the controversy should also be mentioned. Thwing had reservations regarding the giving of complete control to faculties, pointing out that "the history of the government of the two great English universities and their colleges by their own fellows and immediate members has, on

[10] See J. E. Kirkpatrick, *The American College and Its Rulers*, 1926; and Sinclair, *op. cit.*

[11] See H. P. Beck, *Men Who Control Our Universities*, 1947; and A. R. Thompson, "The Professor and the Governing Board," AAUP *Bulletin*, 35:678–687, Winter 1949. C. Eggertsen, who is sympathetic to Beck's position in certain ways, favors some sort of faculty representation in effect, though he does not actually state that such representation should be legal. See "Composition of Governing Boards," in H. Benjamin, ed., *Democracy in the Administration of Higher Education*, 1950, pp. 117–126.

6

the whole, been a history of jealousy, inconsistency, and inefficiency."[12] More recently, Harold Benjamin asserted that boards
of trustees, in spite of their excesses, "have kept the American
University close to the people and have thereby given it a basis
for democratic effectiveness which no *universitas* strictly of mas-
ters or of students could hope to achieve."[13]

Another moderate position was taken in recent writings by
Cowley,[14] who argued that the extent of domination of institutional policy by trustees had been exaggerated and that the cor-
rection of abuses in controlling power did not lie in a radical
change in the formal system of government of American institutions of higher education. In the first place, he pointed out, the
control of such institutions is gradually becoming more diffused,
alumni groups gaining an increasing voice both by establishment
and activation of advisory and visiting boards and by direct representation on governing boards. Second, control by "supra-
academic governments," such as accrediting and state govern-
mental agencies, is increasing. In general, according to Cowley,
the faculties control educational policies, regardless of loudly
publicized exceptions to the rule.

Some writers have rejected changes in legal structure as a solution to problems of college and university government, maintaining that these problems can best be solved through cooperative
processes and through recognition by all parties of their inter-
relatedness and interdependence. This view has its counterpart
in various other fields of administration. Writers such as Follett,
Tead, and Trecker[15] are representative of a group whose work,
with its emphasis on cooperative, functional relationships rather
than on balanced formal power structure, has had an impact on

12 C. F. Thwing, A *History of Higher Education in America*, 1906, pp. 12–13.
13 "The Role of Higher Education in American Democracy," in Benjamin, *op.
cit.*, p. 11.
14 W. H. Cowley, "Professional Growth and Academic Freedom," *Journal of
Higher Education*, 21:225–236, May 1950; "Academic Government," *Educational
Forum*, 15:217, January 1951; "The Government and Administration of Higher
Education: Whence and Whither?," *Journal of the American Association of Collegiate Registrars*, 22:478, July 1947.
15 See M. P. Follett, *Creative Experience*, 1925; O. Tead, *Trustees, Teachers,
Students: Their Role in Higher Education*, 1951, and *The Art of Administration*,
1951; H. B. Trecker, *Group Process in Administration*, 1950.

7

thinking concerning university organization. Shryock's biblio-graphical article, "The Academic Profession in the United States,"[16] while calling attention to the more extreme proposals for change in organization, is tempered by a recognition of the possibilities for trustee-administration-faculty cooperation within existing frameworks.

Newer issues: Scholars, students, citizens— one community

While opposing conceptions concerning the control of institu-tions of higher education have remained largely unresolved, im-portant changes have been occurring in American life from which new questions regarding the faculty member's role in his insti-tution have arisen. During this century institutions of higher education have multiplied in number, and many of them have grown to a size and complexity seldom imagined in earlier days. The practical utility of the scholar's abilities in everyday affairs has received increasing recognition, especially in technological fields. The need for men of learning to share to the full the life of their times, despite the uniqueness of their role in that life, is being expressed in a variety of ways which even Emerson, who urged teachers a hundred years ago to participate more actively in the affairs of their communities, could hardly have dreamed of.

Newer interpretations of the mission of higher education em-phasize its responsibility for relating the activities of the college and university to the needs of society. Obvious implementations of this concept include adult education programs and participa-tion of academic people in cooperative community efforts and activities.

Recognition by institutions of higher education of the need for an increasingly close relationship between the educational pro-gram and the changing needs of society places a new kind of cultural trusteeship on faculty members. Fulfillment of their added responsibilities requires that faculty members, more than ever before, must participate actively in the decisions and opera-tions that set and maintain the course of their college or university.

[16] Shryock, op. cit., p. 70.

Another development affecting the faculty member's professional relationships is the increasing emphasis on the students' stake in the processes of education and in the manner in which their institutions are directed. Hence, the area of faculty-student relationships must be included in any over-all consideration of the rights and obligations of faculty members.[17]

Summarizing this discussion of the role of the faculty member, it may be said that the rights and obligations associated with his various relationships stem from a number of sources. The traditions inherited from European universities, the organizational form higher education has taken in the United States, the increasing material usefulness of certain branches of learning, and various currents of thought in American life, such as the controversial but widespread interest in the vocational "relevance" of liberal arts education, have conditioned the place he holds in society and in his institution. It is understandable that, with rapidly changing conditions, his professional relationships should often be indeterminate or confused. Whatever the factors making for this uncertainty, it lends force to the proposition that the faculty member's role, his rights and obligations, should be clearly formulated and perhaps to some extent legalized.

VIEWS RELATING TO THE FORMALIZATION OF THE FACULTY MEMBER'S ROLE

Opposing views and their adherents

The desire of the academic profession to have the scholar's place understood and respected has occasionally been reflected in an interest in statutory[18] guarantees and other formal assurances from the governing board and administration of the institution. The desire for formalization of the role of the faculty

---

[17] Some writers have urged student participation in the government and administration of their institutions. See F. E. Falvey, *Student Participation in College Administration*, 1952; and H. C. Hand, "Practices in Determining Institutional Objectives," in Benjamin, *op. cit.*, p. 82.

[18] The terms *statute* and *statutory* refer to legislation passed by the governing board or included in the charter. The following definition is observed: "An act of a corporation or of its founder intended as a permanent rule: as, the *statutes* of a university."—*Webster's Collegiate Dictionary* (5th ed.)

9

member has not been unanimous throughout the profession, and the following paragraphs review opinions that have been expressed on the subject as well as factual findings of a number of studies.

The advantages and disadvantages of formalizing in writing the relationships within an institution have been a recurring issue throughout the forty-year period previously described, in which the role of faculties was studied and restudied. The opposing views regarding the value of formal documents in maintaining sound relationships among trustees, administration, and faculty are well illustrated by the two comments quoted below. President A. Lawrence Lowell, in his 1919–20 report to the overseers of Harvard, stated:

. . . the respective functions of the faculties and the governing boards . . . are best learned from experience and embodied in tradition. Tradition has great advantages over regulations. It is a more delicate instrument: it accommodates itself to things which are not susceptible of sharp definition: it is more flexible in its application . . . .[19]

The opposite view was forcefully stated by a recent doctoral student in college administration:

If these opportunities [the opportunities or rights of the members of an enterprise] and the proper methods of their exercise are not explicitly guaranteed, a psychological disadvantage accrues to whoever would exercise those rights. And, in time, any member attempting to exercise those opportunities may find that he must first substantiate his right to do so, which, if founded only upon tradition or memory, may be a hazardous undertaking and jeopardize his status in the group.[20]

[19] Quoted in L. Vold, "Legal Separation of Function in University Organization," *Quarterly Journal of the University of North Dakota*, 10:66, October 1921. The position taken by Lowell was evidently not automatically associated with his office, since his predecessor, Charles William Eliot, had written that "the enactment of statutes which keep in tolerably stable form all these definitions and regulations [on powers of the faculties, and other parts of the regulatory framework] is a weighty part of the duty of the trustees."—*University Administration*, 1908, p. 30.

[20] H. G. Johnshoy, "The Government and Administration of Institutions of Higher Education," 1951, pp. 181–182.

The position of Committee T of the
American Association of University Professors

Committee T of the American Association of University Professors has already been mentioned in connection with its studies of the role of faculties in college and university government. The Committee has been interested also in the place of prescriptive instruments in stabilizing this role; and one aspect of the series of studies it has conducted has been the examination of charters, by-laws, and other documents of academic government. Although the reports of the Committee occasionally support in principle the written formalization of relationships, this support is frequently given with caution, and nowhere does the Committee attempt to set forth its view of the exact place of such documents.

In the Committee's report[21] for 1936 G. H. Sabine, its chairman, acknowledged that legislating into existence new agencies of faculty government could not rule out "the personal equation" and that "organization frequently exists without functioning." In the Committee's 1937 report,[22] in connection with a matter on which only twenty out of one hundred and eighteen institutions had been found to have formal statements, Sabine noted that certain problems were too often matters of personalities, inaccessible to legislation, and that informality was sometimes more democratic than formal regulation. Although the Committee T studies do not establish any particular pattern of formalized principles as generally desirable, there is in some of the reports a suggestion that written formalization may be a help in furthering the climate in which the proper status of the faculty may be achieved. In the 1948 report P. W. Ward noted that the apparent "trend toward the use of written documents defining faculty status . . . may be a factor in improving faculty morale irrespective of its unimportance as a criterion of self-government."[23]

[21] "The Place and Function of Faculties in University Government; Report of Progress of Committee T," G. H. Sabine, Chairman, AAUP *Bulletin*, 22:184, March 1936.

[22] "The Place and Function of Faculties in University Government; Report of Committee T," G. H. Sabine, Chairman, AAUP *Bulletin*, 23:223, March 1937.

[23] "The Role of Faculties in College and University Government," P. W. Ward, Chairman, AAUP *Bulletin*, 34:63, Spring 1948. The 1941 report of the Committee

11

Other studies and other proposals

In addition to the interest in formalization shown by Committee T, independent writers, survey commissions, and other authorities[24] have on occasion stated specifically what matters documents of university government should contain and, in some cases, the processes by which these documents should be drawn up. For example, Verhaalen,[25] in an unpublished doctoral dissertation dealing with organizational problems of public institutions, proposed a standard set of by-laws for a land-grant university enrolling four thousand students. In considering these examples of interest in written instruments of government, it should be recognized that such documents may carry some weight in civil law. Cases have occurred, for example, in which the governing board's own regulations were cited by the court in forcing reinstatement of a discharged faculty member having tenure.[26] Regulations of the board, in at least one instance, were held to become part of the appointee's contract. However, it has been pointed out that courts also tend to enforce custom in the absence of any contrary criteria of law.[27]

included a classified list of the various types of formal documents used in the institutions the Committee had studied. See "The Place and Function of Faculties in University and College Government; Report of Committee T," P. W. Ward, Chairman, AAUP *Bulletin*, 27:161–162, April 1941.

[24] See, for example, E. C. Elliott, M. M. Chambers, and W. A. Ashbrook, *The Government of Higher Education*, 1935, pp. 99–105; American Council on Education, *Louisiana State University, A Survey Report*, 1940, pp. 10, 24–37; L. S. Woodburne and N. P. Meade, *An Appraisal of the Faculty Organization By-Laws Governing the College of the City of New York*, September 1, 1950.

[25] R. J. Verhaalen, "Legislation and Higher Education: Laws and By-Laws Affecting the Government of Public Institutions of Higher Learning," 1948.

[26] See Ironside *v.* Tead, (N.Y. Misc.), 13 N.Y.S. (2d) 17 (1939); and State *ex. rel.* Keeney *v.* Ayers, (Mont.), 92 P. (2d) 306 (1939). The former case concerned an instructor in economics at Brooklyn College; the latter, the librarian, with professorial status, at Montana State University. Both cited in M. M. Chambers, *The Colleges and the Courts, 1936–40*, 1941, pp. 24–26.

[27] M. M. Chambers, "Municipal University Business," *College and University Business*, 3:23, September 1947.

THE STARTING POINT: A TENTATIVE BODY
OF PRINCIPLES AND PRACTICES

Arguments cited for and against written formalization of the faculty member's rights and obligations have been perhaps too often concerned with statutes, rules, and regulations in general, without regard to the merits of particular provisions in particular circumstances. For the purpose at hand, therefore, the general topic of faculty rights and obligations had to be broken down into specific provisions found to exist, which could be studied in their respective contexts.

The first step toward this breakdown was to define the terms *rights* and *obligations.* The ultimate question of what the rights and obligations of individuals or groups are or should be is a metaphysical one, and clearly beyond the scope of this undertaking. Furthermore, they exist in various degrees, ranging from logical expectation to moral commitment. Some rights, too, are effective but indeterminate; as one scholar observed, privileges exist in academic life that, if claimed as rights, are likely to be lost.

Since the interest of the study embraced all these qualities and degrees of the faculty member's rights and obligations, it was found practical to define them as "those expectations of and by the faculty member that are recognized by his institution as reasonable." That is, regardless of the legal enforceability of a principle, if it is clearly recognized in any way as a reasonable expectation, this study is concerned with it, even though the formality of recognition may vary from the statutory enactments of the governing board to the sometimes unwritten but binding rules that can be such strong regulatory forces within a college. Throughout this book a guarantee based on trustee legislation will be regarded as more formal than one based on an act of some person or group less clearly authorized to make such a guarantee. A written commitment, moreover, will be considered more formal than one based only on unwritten understanding. Formalization, in other words, is a relative matter, though one in respect to which

13

sharp contrasts will be apparent among certain institutions to be discussed.

The organizational framework of the study, already referred to as the Academic Bill of Rights and Obligations, was developed as a means of making data from eight institutions comparable. First a list was made of all the subjects dealt with in the documents of government of a variety of colleges and universities, both within and outside of the group to be studied, that could be construed as pertaining to the rights and obligations of faculty members. The provisions thus listed were then reduced to a single set of concepts or principles, each of which might be found expressed in one or more specific policies or practices.

This initial framework, which was used in studying each of the eight colleges, was gradually modified to accommodate additional concepts and practices encountered as the study progressed. The resulting Academic Bill of Rights and Obligations appears on pages 14–18 and provides the headings for the Comparative Synopsis, which begins on page 124. The original purpose of this outline was to serve as a topical guide to an inquiry. Its use does not imply any presumption as to its validity as an authoritative document on academic government. In the course of the project, however, the author did arrive at certain conclusions regarding the practical utility of such an instrument for the determination of policies and procedures, and these opinions are presented in the closing chapter.

AN ACADEMIC BILL OF RIGHTS AND OBLIGATIONS

Outline of Principles and Related Practices

PART I: Rights and obligations relating to personal and professional status

Principle 1: The right and the obligation to be governed by clear and mutually binding terms of appointment.

1-*a.* Formalization of appointment by contract or other written commitment.

Principle 2: The right to an understanding of the conditions governing duration of appointment and chances for promotion.

14

2-*a*. Statement of qualifications for appointment and promotion to each rank.

2-*b*. Statement of policies governing duration of appointment.

Principle 3: The right to fair and objective processes in matters of reappointment, promotion, and increase in salary.

3-*a*. Principal processes recognized in effecting an appointment or reappointment.

3-*b*. Principal processes recognized in effecting a promotion or increase in salary.

Principle 4: The right to achieve continuous tenure after sufficient time to prove oneself.

4-*a*. Explicit recognition of continuous tenure as a principle.

4-*b*. Designation of ranks that, under the recognized rules, may achieve continuous tenure.

4-*c*. Provisions governing length of probationary period preceding continuous tenure.

4-*d*. Limitation of right of continuous tenure: Circumstances of the institution under which tenure may become invalid.

4-*e*. Other qualifications and interpretations relating to the right of continuous tenure.

Principle 5: The right to advance notice of non-reappointment or dismissal, and the obligation to give advance notice of voluntary resignation.

5-*a*. Provisions for advance notice of non-reappointment.

5-*b*. Requirements of appointee regarding notice of resignation.

5-*c*. Specification of interval required for dismissal to take effect.

Principle 6: The right to some "due process" to assure fairness in case of non-reappointment or dismissal.

6-*a*. Processes designed to assure fairness in decision of non-reappointment.

6-*b*. Definition of grounds for dismissal.

6-*c*. Requirement of formal statement of charges, if the teacher requests it, in dismissal proceedings.

6-*d*. Guarantee of a hearing, if the teacher requests it, before decision to dismiss is made.

6-*e*. Guarantee of a further hearing before a higher authority, if the teacher appeals.

6-*f*. Action required to make dismissal final.

6-*g*. Guarantee of an equitable salary settlement in case of dismissal.

Principle 7: The right to be governed by a salary policy that is understood, consistent, and determined in the light of consultation with those affected by it.

7-*a*. Existence of a published salary scale.

15

7-*b*. Faculty participation in the shaping of salary policy.

7-*c*. Provisions concerning upper salary limits of each rank and conformity to scale.

Principle 8: The right to such assistance in matters of personal and family responsibility as the institution is in a position to provide, and the obligation to avail oneself of such help as may forestall one's ever becoming an economic liability, moral or legal, of the institution.

8-*a*. Privileges and obligations in matters of housing.

8-*b*. Optional and required participation in insurance, retirement, and other plans to meet personal risks.

8-*c*. An objectively determined time of retirement.

8-*d*. Miscellaneous other privileges.

PART II: Rights and obligations relating to personal and professional freedom and growth

Principle 9: The right to encouragement and protection in the activities appropriate to a member of a professional body dedicated to the search for and dissemination of truth, and the obligations associated with this right.

9-*a*. Guarantees relating to academic freedom in general.

9-*b*. Qualifications and obligations relating to the guarantee of academic freedom.

9-*c*. Provisions governing outside employment while on appointment at the institution.

9-*d*. Provisions governing absence from campus during academic year.

Principle 10: The right to equal consideration with others, regardless of creed in religious or other matters.

10-*a*. Regulations regarding loyalty oaths.

10-*b*. Guarantee of religious freedom and equality.

Principle 11: The right to assistance from the institution, through sabbatical leave or other means, in furthering one's development as a professional person, and the obligations associated with receipt of such assistance.

11-*a*. Designation of persons who may obtain sabbatical leave.

11-*b*. Provisions for equitable awarding of sabbatical leave.

11-*c*. Stated or understood obligations associated with award of sabbatical leave.

11-*d*. Provisions for travel allowances or grants to attend professional meetings.

11-*e*. Provisions for other assistance in efforts toward professional growth.

Principle 12: The obligation to exercise one's professional freedom

16

within the limits of service to the educational enterprise of which one is a member.

12-*a.* Provisions governing adherence to academic schedule.

12-*b.* Provisions governing maintenance of academic standards and purposes.

Principle 13: The obligation to observe duly the rights and responsibilities of students.

13-*a.* The obligation to be as fair as possible in evaluating students' academic work and in determining a student's academic status.

13-*b.* Provisions governing faculty members' responsibilities in handling cases of academic dishonesty.

13-*c.* Provisions governing the giving of help to individual students.

PART III: Rights and obligations relating to the faculty member's share in directing the educational enterprise

Principle 14: The right to work in a departmental or divisional unit that is reasonably free from the arbitrary domination of an individual or a limited group.

14-*a.* Manner of selection and term of tenure of department chairman (and of division chairman if the latter has major administrative responsibilities).

14-*b.* Participation of department members in decisions on appointments and promotions.

14-*c.* Participation of department members in the direction of other affairs of the department.

14-*d.* Provisions designed to assure equitable distribution of the teaching load.

Principle 15: The right and the obligation to play a responsible role in the over-all functions appropriate to a college faculty.

15-*a.* Definition of the responsibility and the authority of the faculty as a whole.

15-*b.* Definition of faculty membership.

15-*c.* Definition of voting rights.

15-*d.* Frequency of faculty meetings.

15-*e.* Guaranteed rights of participation in faculty deliberations.

15-*f.* Provision for fair representation on faculty policy-making, administrative, and judicial committees.

15-*g.* Restrictions and qualifications affecting individual eligibility for membership in faculty policy-making, administrative, and judicial committees.

15-*h.* Provision for direct access by faculty members to faculty policy-making, administrative, and judicial committees.

17

Principle 16: The right to a direct means of communication with the governing board of the institution.

16-*a*. Provisions for faculty conference with, or representation on, the governing board.

16-*b*. Provisions for faculty participation in the choice of principal officers of the institution.

CHAPTER II

COMPARISON OF
THE EIGHT COLLEGES

PRINCIPAL DOCUMENTS

As was observed in the preceding chapter, the formality of recognition given to rights and obligations may vary in degree from published trustee legislation to unwritten though consciously formulated practices. The comparisons made in this chapter between practices in the different institutions, therefore, will take account of all degrees of official recognition accorded each principle in the Academic Bill of Rights and Obligations. As a starting point, however, it will be useful to examine the various kinds of written instruments in which these principles are embodied, and for this purpose a list of the most important documents studied is given in Table 1.

It will be noted that although every governing board has by-laws, the by-laws do not contain all the board legislation concerning faculty rights and obligations. Hobart College, having only one published body of board legislation, is an apparent exception to this generalization, but the reason is that Hobart had not, at the time of this study, completed its codification of rules relating

TABLE 1

Principal College Documents* Studied, and Source of Authority for Rights and Obligations Included

Institution and Documents	Regulations by Governing Board	Regulations by Faculty	Regulations by Administration	Official Interpretation of Principles Established by Usage	Regulations by Other Authority
COLGATE					
By-Laws of the Board of Trustees	x				
Faculty Handbook	x	x	x	x	
HAVERFORD					
By-Laws of the Corporation**	x				
Information for Members of the Faculty	x	x	x		
HOBART					
By-Laws of the Colleges of the Seneca	x				
MOUNT HOLYOKE					
By-Laws of the Trustees of Mount Holyoke College	x				
Handbook of Faculty Legislation and Related Information	x	x		x	
SARAH LAWRENCE					
Sarah Lawrence College By-Laws	x				
Faculty By-Laws		x			
"Statement of Principles and Procedures," prepared by Faculty Planning Committee and accepted by the Board of Trustees, April 12, 1945	x	x		x	
"To the Students, Faculty, and Alumnae Council of Sarah Lawrence College," letter from the President and the Chairman of the Board, January 18, 1952 (statement on academic freedom)	x				
SWARTHMORE					
By-Laws of the Corporation	x				
Faculty Regulations	x	x	x		
VASSAR					
Governance of Vassar College:					
By-Laws of the Board of Trustees	x				
Principles Underlying Relations of Trustees and Faculty	x				
Academic Statute	x	x			
WESLEYAN					
By-Laws of Wesleyan University	x				
By-Laws of the Academic Council	x				x

* Other than charters and documents concerned primarily with student programs, student affairs, and routine information. For the sake of simplicity and emphasis, the names of all documents that have recognized titles are italicized, both here and throughout the book, although many of them are in mimeographed form.

** Contained in *Act of Incorporation, Supplements, and Amendments; By-Laws,* November 1, 1932.

20

to the faculty. Much legislation affecting the Hobart faculty is contained in the minutes of board and faculty meetings.

The scope of provisions contained in the trustee by-laws varies widely among the eight institutions, as previous studies[1] have shown. There is no single area of faculty rights and obligations that is dealt with in the by-laws of all eight governing boards. Matters treated in several of them, however, are (1) definition of faculty membership; (2) definition of the responsibility and the authority of the faculty; (3) relationship between board and faculty; and (4) appointment and promotion procedures. Actually, the contents of the by-laws indicate merely what the term *by-laws* means to the respective governing bodies, assuming that they have a definite concept.

Other important trustee legislation affecting faculty rights and obligations may be set forth by the board in additional codes (for example, the second and third sections of the *Governance of Vassar College*), or in other compilations of rules by the administration or the faculty. In the latter case, of course, it may be difficult to determine whether a regulation originated with the board or elsewhere. The Appendix of the Mount Holyoke *Handbook of Faculty Legislation and Related Information*, for example, contains a number of important but undocumented provisions.

Only in the three women's colleges does the faculty systematically codify its own legislation. Although the *By-Laws of the Academic Council*, at Wesleyan, deal with many of the same subjects as the formal documents of the faculty at Mount Holyoke, Sarah Lawrence, and Vassar, the Wesleyan code is a product, not of the faculty as a whole, but of the senior faculty (consisting of full professors and top administrative officers) alone. Swarthmore does have a booklet entitled *Faculty Regulations*, but this is an editing of faculty records by the secretary of the faculty rather than a formal code, and, except for the 1924 "Joint Resolution Concerning Faculty Tenure," it contains little of relevance to this study.

The documents described above will be referred to throughout this chapter, which is devoted to a comparative examination of

---

[1] See E. C. Elliott, M. M. Chambers, and W. A. Ashbrook, *The Government of Higher Education*, 1935, pp. 99–105.

the eight institutions with respect to their recognition of faculty rights and obligations. The order of treatment is that given in the Academic Bill of Rights and Obligations at the close of Chapter I.

CONDITIONS OF APPOINTMENT
AND PROMOTION

Principle 1: The right and the obligation to be governed by clear and mutually binding terms of appointment

ITEM 1-A. *Formalization of appointment by contract or other written commitment.*—All eight institutions recognize faculty appointments in writing, though there is wide variation in the extent of prescription requiring this practice. Colgate, Haverford, and Vassar have trustee legislation calling for a written mutual understanding of the terms of appointment. The others have policies similar to those called for in the Colgate, Haverford, and Vassar legislation, though some have no trustee prescription as to what a contractual document should contain, and others—for example, Swarthmore—have no legislation requiring the existence of a contract. Some faculty members in one institution did not consider themselves to have a contract, though none thought that it mattered whether they had one or not. The opinion was frequently encountered, among administrative officers and members of committees concerned with faculty appointments, that a faculty member was never held to his commitment to complete his term of service, even if under contractual obligation to do so. The institution, it was said, never prevented an appointee from taking advantage of a more desirable offer elsewhere.[2]

Principle 2: The right to an understanding of the conditions governing duration of appointment and chances for promotion

ITEM 2-A. *Statement of qualifications for appointment and promotion to each rank.*—There is wide variation among the eight institutions with respect to the statement of qualifications for ap-

2 Further discussion of this finding is included in connection with Item 5-*b* (see p. 36).

pointment and promotion. Most formal and explicit are Colgate and Vassar, both of which have codified trustee legislation that attempts to define the qualities and accomplishments expected of members of each rank. Among the other colleges it was occasionally said that written standards for appointment and promotion, not being susceptible of objective application, would have to be expressed in very general terms, and that it was preferable, therefore, not to have any. If the rules were sufficiently specific to be useful as a guide, they would also be inflexible just when sound subjective judgment about a person was required.

One comment from a junior faculty member seems pertinent in this connection because it was made concerning an institution whose administrative pattern and personnel were generally praised. It was informally understood, he said, that teaching ability ranked foremost among the qualities considered in judging a member's fitness for advancement, and nobody questioned the good faith of the administration in this insistence. There was a group of faculty members, however, who disagreed strongly with the administration's apparent concept of what effective teaching was.

A different source of faculty insecurity in the area of appointment and promotion was revealed in two other institutions that make no attempt to define criteria for promotion, except that one requires a doctoral degree for any professorial rank. The feeling was expressed that it was uncomfortable "not to know where you stand." In talking with persons who expressed this view, the writer sometimes asked the faculty member to distinguish between that insecurity which was inherent in being on probation and that which he felt was added unnecessarily by the failure of the college to commit itself to a statement of what was expected of him. One person said: "I don't know; maybe you can never get promoted."

An effort was made by the writer to determine to what extent faculty members felt that criteria for promotion had to be in statutory or at least written form in order to be considered perfectly clear. There was definite consensus on this point among those interviewed; the faculty members who particularly looked

23

for greater clarity than already existed generally conceded that the administration's word in any form would be sufficient assurance if standards were only made explicit.

ITEM 2-B. *Statement of policies governing duration of appointment.*—Policies governing the length of each term of appointment, whether codified or merely understood, presented a confusing subject of inquiry in several institutions, either because of the complexity of the policy or because its transient nature led to conflicting interpretations of what the policy and even the practice were at a given time.

The policies governing duration of appointments are, of course, subject to the pressure of outside conditions. One college, which once had a stated policy of two-year appointments for instructors, was reluctant to continue this policy during a recent period of uncertain enrollments and other budgetary difficulties. The trustees accordingly initiated a one-year appointment policy, which caused the junior faculty members so much concern that an incomplete effort was made to return to the two-year rule. Understandably, the facts of present practice are a matter of disagreement.

One difficulty in relating to actual practice the stated policies governing duration of appointment was the frequently elastic wording of the policies themselves. Numerous exceptions and qualifications appear in the policies as they are reported in the Comparative Synopsis.

Principle 3: The right to fair and objective processes in matters of reappointment, promotion, and increase in salary

ITEMS 3-A AND 3-B. *Principal processes recognized in effecting appointment, reappointment, promotion, or increase in salary.*— In considering the processes of reappointment and advancement as they relate to the over-all topic, it seemed especially important to distinguish between practices that were clearly statutory and required and those that, although not thus formalized, were nevertheless significant. From the Comparative Synopsis (pp. 129–132) it will be seen that most of the eight colleges have few guarantees of fairness to the individual appointee that have the formal stand-

24

ing of a trustee statute. All of them, however, do have established procedures that, allegedly, no chief administrative officer could disregard without endangering his relationship with his faculty.

Only three of the colleges—Mount Holyoke, Vassar, and Wesleyan—have codified trustee legislation requiring the president to consult anyone except the board of trustees regarding appointment recommendations. Sarah Lawrence might be considered to belong to this group, since the *Faculty By-Laws* do call for consultation procedures, and the fact that these by-laws are accepted by the board might be taken to mean that they are the equivalent of board legislation. (This, however, was not the impression of at least one administrative officer consulted.) Because of the recognition by all eight colleges, however, that a president must follow certain consultative procedures in matters of appointment, reappointment, promotion, and salary, the legal provisions are of less importance to the individuals concerned than the accepted principles and practices.

Decisions concerning reappointment and advancement are made by (1) the president and (2) the people who advise the president. Where the decision is usually a group action, as it is in several of the colleges where faculty advisory committees operate, the people who advise the advisory group also influence the decision. If, as is postulated here, the individual concerned has the right to have decisions about his appointment and promotion made in as objective a manner as possible, there must be provisions to assure that the most pertinent facts and opinions about him will be considered. It may be the president who determines what the sources of the most pertinent facts and opinions are, as at Swarthmore; or, at the other extreme, the individual himself may be permitted to name the people to be consulted, as at Sarah Lawrence in case of impending termination of appointment (see Comparative Synopsis, Item 6-a).

Between these two extremes lie a variety of practices. Most frequently it is the department chairman who has the decisive voice in matters of appointment, reappointment, and advancement. Even where powerful elected committees exist to advise on appointments, there is sometimes so strong a reluctance to override a department chairman that some junior faculty members feel that the advisory committee is a less vigorous force for justice than the senior members of the faculty say it is. This feeling was strongly stated at least once in two of the five colleges that have such advisory committees, and there were signs of a similar feeling in one or two of the others.

Of the institutions that have no standing advisory committees on appointment matters, Colgate is interesting because of the lack of any apparent feeling among the faculty that there ought to be such a committee (see p. 77). One of the division directors at Colgate said that a faculty advisory committee "would become a log-rolling device." Whether "log-rolling" is a fair description of the operation of any of the advisory committees in the other colleges is questionable, but some faculty members familiar with them believe that it is.

No sharp divergence of opinion appears about whether there should be broad consultation on appointment matters, all institutions seeming to take consultation for granted whether or not there is standing machinery to provide for it. When salary raises are considered apart from the question of promotion, however, differences of opinion and practice appear. The extent of faculty participation in awarding individual salary raises seems to be greatest at Sarah Lawrence, where the Advisory Committee on Appointments in effect determines salaries jointly with the president. It should be pointed out, of course, that since Sarah Lawrence does not have separate faculty ranks, the salary status of each individual serves to some extent as recognition comparable to advancement in rank at other institutions. Some participation of faculty members other than administrative officers in individual salary matters is common in a number of other institutions, notably Hobart, where the Advisory Council, composed of administrative officers and elected professors, regularly considers the salaries of colleagues below the rank of professor. Faculty members at still other institutions, however, such as Wesleyan and Mount Holyoke, were emphatic in pointing out that their elected advisory bodies did not consider individual salaries. The question of faculty participation in formulating salary policy *in general* is considered in connection with Principle 7.

26

In most colleges of the group the strength of a teacher's bargaining position was alleged by some to be of considerable importance in determining reappointment and advancement. Personnel at several institutions recalled former regimes that had kept faculty members in a junior instructional rank for many years because nothing had forced attention upon the discrepancy between their status and their merits. This complaint was not made of any of the present administrations, though in at least two institutions there were criticisms of the extent and the objectivity of reviews of individual records. There are really two questions with respect to such reviews: first, when they are to be carried out; second, how they are to be carried out. If a college gives only term appointments, even to people who have in effect continuous tenure, it is almost inevitable that some consideration of the person's value to the institution will take place at renewal time. If, however, people with continuous tenure do not receive term appointments, it is presumably easier to forget about them as individuals who are striving to better themselves. For this reason, Vassar has a statute that requires the Advisory Committee to consider, at least every five years, the advancement in rank of associate professors at maximum salary and an increase in salary for full professors below the top of the scale.

CONDITIONS OF TENURE AND SEPARATION

Principle 4: The right to achieve continuous tenure after sufficient time to prove oneself

For purposes of this study, *continuous tenure* was the term chosen to designate the guarantee of continuous appointment until retirement, subject to termination only under conditions mutually understood and agreed upon. Although not all the institutions studied use this term, the various designations they employ, such as *tenure, permanent tenure,* and *indefinite tenure,* seem to have the same meaning for practical purposes.

As will be shown, there is considerable variation in the formality with which continuous tenure is guaranteed, and also in the percentage of faculty members who manage to attain it (see Table 2).

27

TABLE 2

ATTAINMENT OF CONTINUOUS TENURE BY FACULTY MEMBERS*

Rank	Distribution of Faculty Membership, by Ranks		Attainment of Continuous Tenure, by Ranks		
	Number of Faculty in Each Rank	Per Cent of Faculty in Each Rank	Number of Each Rank with Tenure	Per Cent of Each Rank with Tenure	Per Cent of All Tenure Holders in Each Rank
COLGATE					
Professors	43	40	41	95	67
Associate Professors	19	18	18	95	30
Assistant Professors	28	26	2	7	3
Instructors	17	16	0	0	0
Total	107	100	61	57	100
HAVERFORD					
Professors	16	35	16	100	55
Associate Professors	15	32	13	87	45
Assistant Professors	10	22	0	0	0
Instructors	5	11	0	0	0
Total	46	100	29	63	100
HOBART					
Professors	14	25	14	100	56
Associate Professors	5	9	5	100	20
Assistant Professors	20	36	5	25	20
Instructors	17	30	1	6	4
Total	56	100	25	45	100
MOUNT HOLYOKE					
Professors	42	32	42	100	50
Associate Professors	37	28	35	95	42

Assistant Professors	27	20	6	22	7
Instructors	26	20	1	4	1
Total	132	100	84	64	100
SARAH LAWRENCE					
Total (No academic ranks)	43	100	30	70	
SWARTHMORE					
Professors	28	30	26	93	40
Associate Professors	34	37	33	97	51
Assistant Professors	25	27	6	24	9
Instructors	6	6	0	0	0
Total	93	100	65	70	100
VASSAR					
Professors	51	33	44	86	79
Associate Professors	30	19	12	40	21
Assistant Professors	27	17	0	0	0
Instructors	49	31	0	0	0
Total	157	100	56	36	100
WESLEYAN					
Professors	31	36	31	100	60
Associate Professors	20	23	19	95	36
Assistant Professors	20	23	2	10	4
Instructors	16	18	0	0	0
Total	87	100	52	60	100

Continuous tenure is defined as expectation of continuous appointment until retirement, to be terminated only under conditions fully covered by mutually understood provisions. This table includes only teaching faculty members in the regular instructional ranks who are on full-time appointment. (In the case of Sarah Lawrence, where there are no ranks, it includes all teaching faculty members on full-time appointment.) It does not include persons having the title of lecturer or other special designation, or members who are primarily administrative officers.

ITEM 4-A. *Explicit recognition of continuous tenure as a principle.*—Three colleges—Colgate, Haverford, and Vassar—have complete codes relating to continuous tenure, while Hobart, Mount Holyoke, and Swarthmore have a combination of legislation and firmly established policies that go beyond the legislation. Sarah Lawrence and Wesleyan have no written embodiment of tenure policies, but such policies are said to be operative and fully understood. In all eight institutions the major implications of the AAUP–AAC *Principles* seem to be accepted, if not explicitly incorporated in the documents of government. Certain departures from the AAUP–AAC position will be pointed out presently.

ITEM 4-B. *Designation of ranks that, under the recognized rules, may achieve continuous tenure.*—The data that have been assembled in Table 2 regarding the number of teachers in each rank who do achieve tenure[3] pertain only to full-time members of the teaching faculty who are not primarily administrative officers. Although there are teachers with tenure who are not included in this group, to include all classes of appointees in which there are tenure-holders could give the figures a false meaning, because of the various types of special appointments that exist in some of the colleges. The purpose of Table 2 is merely to show the relative attainability of continuous tenure for the *average* faculty member.

In principle all eight colleges extend the opportunity of obtaining continuous tenure to professors and associate professors, although the ease with which tenure is obtainable varies from one college to another. Nearly all professors and associate professors in seven of the colleges actually do have tenure, as Table 2 shows. The exception is Vassar, where 14 per cent of the professors and 60 per cent of the associate professors do not have tenure.

Recognition of the principle of tenure for assistant professors varies widely, from colleges where the "up-or-out" promotion policy obtains, as at Wesleyan (stated in *By-Laws of the Aca-*

[3] The term *tenure* is used from time to time throughout this book in place of *continuous tenure*, where no ambiguity will result from such use.

demic Council; see Comparative Synopsis, Item 2-*b*), to colleges where the assistant professorship may be a terminal rank. At Hobart, for example, one fourth of the full-time assistant professors have tenure, while Wesleyan's policy tends to prevent their being kept in that rank beyond the specified probationary period. An intermediate position is exemplified by Haverford, where an assistant professor who is under forty years of age is not necessarily given tenure, but may receive it by special action of the board of managers. The granting of continuous tenure to instructors is not a generally recognized practice in any of the eight colleges, though in several it is possible for an instructor to achieve it simply by serving the probationary time. This is true at Hobart and Mount Holyoke, whereas it is contrary to policy at Swarthmore and Vassar. (One member of the Swarthmore faculty, however, did have tenure while he was an instructor, and it was said that this situation might occur again under exceptional conditions.) None of the colleges, however, except in special circumstances, keeps teachers indefinitely as instructors, and the cases noted in Table 2 include such faculty members as physical education instructors, to whom, it seems, normal promotion procedures do not usually apply. Colgate specifically excepts physical education teachers from tenure provisions, making their tenure subject to special action by the governing board in every case.

Table 2 shows that a smaller percentage of the full-time instructional ranks achieve continuous tenure at Vassar than at the other seven institutions, the total of 36 per cent representing only about half the proportion attaining tenure at Sarah Lawrence and at Swarthmore, where the figure is 70 per cent. The percentage of appointees with continuous tenure depends partly, of course, on the percentage of appointees in the two senior ranks, and this is especially so at Vassar, where the two junior ranks are not eligible for continuous tenure. Furthermore, even in institutions where assistant professors and instructors may in principle achieve tenure, other policies and conditions operate to prevent them from doing so, or at least to keep the percentage of those who do succeed very low. The figures on attainment of

31

tenure by the total membership of the various faculties, therefore, are not as significant as the figures for the separate ranks, for the total percentage is greatly influenced by the rank distribution—that is, by the relative seniority of the faculty.

It may be said in passing that concern was expressed in at least two institutions about the increasing "top-heaviness" of the faculty in rank distribution. This condition was noted as having serious implications both for the morale of junior members and for the salary budget. Rough quotas of rank distribution in the several departments seemed to exist in some colleges, but these quotas were not rigid or formalized. The dean of one faculty stated that small institutions could not reasonably employ a quota system in the strict sense.

ITEM 4-C. *Provisions governing length of probationary period preceding continuous tenure.*—All eight institutions appear to accept seven years or less as the maximum probationary period, though it is sometimes not clear whether the period intended is actually seven years or anything up to but not including the seventh year. Colgate explicitly states that tenure is conferred by any appointment for the *eighth* year of service, so that seven years is the maximum probationary period there. At Hobart and Swarthmore, however, an appointment for the *seventh* year of service is considered to confer tenure, so that the probationary period there is in effect six years.

In all eight colleges, however, the effective probationary period is often shorter, because of a variety of factors, than that which is formally prescribed. For full professors the period is normally waived entirely at Haverford and Wesleyan, and it is shortened by varying amounts in the other colleges, as it tends to be for associate professors as well. The sequence of term appointments is another factor that shortens the effective probationary period in several colleges. For example, as the Comparative Synopsis shows, an appointment for the fifth year at Sarah Lawrence, if it is a four-year appointment, will confer tenure because it will outlast the probationary period. Only two colleges, Colgate and Mount Holyoke, have a formal provision permitting the transfer of three years of probationary service from another institution, in accordance with the AAUP–AAC *Principles.*

32

ITEM 4-D. *Limitation of right of continuous tenure: Circumstances of the institution under which tenure may become invalid.*
—Half of the colleges have explicit trustee legislation defining the circumstances under which the institution can be relieved of its continuous tenure commitment. The others have either blanket endorsement of the AAUP–AAC *Principles,* as does Mount Holyoke, or unwritten understandings that these principles apply, as does Sarah Lawrence. Because of the infrequency with which appointments of faculty members with continuous tenure are terminated, it is difficult to ascertain the practical significance of the provisions found. Most of the colleges seem to be reluctant to take such action except in extreme circumstances.

Because of the variety of conditions under which faculty members are separated from service, and because of the lack of common terminology among the colleges regarding the circumstances of separation, it has been found desirable for purposes of the following discussion to classify the various possible separation actions. This classification, which is based on descriptive terms designed to facilitate discussion, appears in Table 3.

Termination of service because of financial exigencies of the college is recognized as legitimate, but it is uncertain whether a term appointment can be broken for this reason. One administrative officer said that in his college people with term appointments would be let go before those with permanent appointments and that it would be considered legitimate to break a term appointment in effecting the separation. None of those interviewed, however, thought this would ever occur.

Termination of service due to a change in the educational program that reduces the need for certain professional services is also generally accepted, and a number of instances of its happening were mentioned. The event had been a controversial one in at least one case, since the concept "change in educational program" is a relative one, and a new orientation in departmental plans or a new emphasis on an interdisciplinary unit of the curriculum may or may not terminate the usefulness of a department member. In the controversial case just mentioned, a member of a large and important department was released on the grounds that the department was developing new plans outside his field

33

TABLE 3

CLASSIFICATION OF CONDITIONS OF SEPARATION FROM SERVICE, OTHER THAN RETIREMENT

Type of Separation	Circumstances	Reasons	Time
Resignation	Resignation voluntary	On faculty member's own initiative	Usually with a required period of notice from faculty member, either stated or understood
	Resignation induced	To save the faculty member or the institution from the adverse consequences of an airing of their mutual difficulty	Time and other terms as negotiated in each case
	Resignation forced	As an alternative to formal dismissal: an option for the sake of dignity and privacy (on both sides) when clear grounds for dismissal exist	
Separation by Necessity	Separation forced because of conditions of the institution	Because of financial exigencies Because of change of educational program	May occur 1. At expiration of appointment 2. During term of appointment 3. During continuous appointment, whether with tenure or subject to termination on notice
Simple Non-reappointment	Expiration of the faculty member's term without renewal, tenure rights not being involved	No formal cause required	Only at end of term, presumably with a period of notice to the person involved
Dismissal (including non-reappointment in spite of continuous tenure	Forced termination of service when person has, or is presumed to have, continuous tenure Forced termination of service during the person's term appointment and not (a circumstance which may coincide with that of the item above	For definite *cause*, attributable to the *appointee himself* (as opposed to other reasons for forced separation)	May occur 1. Immediately or soon after decision 2. After required time interval 3. Immediately, but with a period of continued salary payment

of specialization. This action would probably be questioned by colleges whose documents of government stipulate, as those of Haverford do, that every effort must be made to find a way to use the professional services of the faculty member concerned. It would also be questioned by colleges that require a five-year delay before such action can take effect, as Vassar does, in order to enable the displaced scholar, if competent, to come abreast of the new development. One of the most liberal provisions concerning such dislocations is that of Haverford, where separation under the circumstances described above carries the right of two years' notice with full salary.

ITEM 4-E. *Other qualifications and interpretations relating to the right of continuous tenure.*—Item 4-*e* was included as a separate item in the Academic Bill of Rights and Obligations only to record certain provisions that seem to merit presentation but that cannot be considered on a comparative basis because the information is not complete for all colleges visited. For example, the Colgate provision stating that the division of physical education is not governed by tenure rules may exist in a less formal way in other colleges of the group. Whether or not time spent on leave is counted as part of the probationary period is clearly stated in some colleges but is a matter of disagreement or uncertainty in others.

The question whether attainment of the associate professorship is considered primarily a recognition of progress, as at Wesleyan (see Comparative Synopsis, Item 2-*b*), or a final promotion, as it may be at Vassar,[4] would seem to be an important one, from the point of view of the faculty member's right to an understanding of his place and to a feeling of dignity in moderate achievement. Whether the acceptance of second-rank recognition as a mark of creditable achievement can be fostered by legislative action is, of course, debatable.

One provision in this miscellaneous group that deserves mention is the Colgate guarantee that future revisions of tenure poli-

---

[4] "The associate professorship may be appropriately regarded as a post suitable to one's lifework. . . . Members of the faculty of the rank of professor shall have achieved marked distinction as scholars or as teachers."—*Academic Statute*, Art. X, sec. 2A, (4)(5), in *Governance of Vassar College.*

cies will not deprive anyone of tenure earned under present rules. This is the only formal provision of its kind among the eight colleges, and the extent to which this principle is assumed in the other seven is uncertain.

Principle 5: The right to advance notice of non-reappointment or dismissal, and the obligation to give advance notice of resignation

ITEM 5-A. *Provisions for advance notice of non-reappointment.*—There was considerable variation among the eight colleges in the advance notice given of non-reappointment, and, especially for one-year appointments, considerable discrepancy between stated policy and practice. At least two institutions that have formal policies requiring six months' notice to one-year appointees delay their final decisions until the spring, when the enrollment picture for the following fall is clearer. Except in the case of one-year appointments, the policies seem to be well observed, and many administrators were said to make an effort to give earlier notice than the formal policy called for. At least one instance was cited of a reappointment that had been made because the faculty member had not been formally advised, within the specified period, that his service was to be terminated.

ITEM 5-B. *Requirements of appointee regarding notice of resignation.*—Five of the colleges have formal requirements relating to advance notice of resignation. The provisions at Colgate are the most extensive, following closely the American Association of University Professors' 1929 "Statement Concerning Resignations,"[5] although this document is not specifically referred to. In spite of the explicit requirements of these institutions, the comment was frequently made that such requirements did not prevent faculty members from asking for release on inconveniently short notice. Moreover, the writer heard of no case in which the release was not granted. The feeling of administrative officers and faculty members involved in administration seemed to be that, in practice, all the obligations are with the institution in this matter.

[5] In "Academic Freedom and Tenure: Statements of Principles," AAUP *Bulletin*, 38:122, Spring 1952.

ITEM 5-C. *Specification of interval required for dismissal to take effect.*—The term *dismissal*, as used in this study, is confined to termination of appointment on the college's initiative (see Table 3), presumably for reasons discreditable to the appointee. Five of the eight colleges have some written provision either for advance notice of dismissal or for a period of salary continuation in the event of dismissal for reasons other than those concerning morality. Since dismissal, in the sense in which the term is used here, has not occurred more than half a dozen times in the entire group of colleges in twenty-five years, to the best knowledge of the officers consulted, there was little opportunity to investigate the operation of this type of provision.

Principle 6: The right to some "due process" to assure fairness in case of non-reappointment or dismissal

The distinctions made in Table 3 among the various conditions of separation had to be kept in mind in examining the provisions of the eight colleges and the expressed views of college officers regarding fair processes of termination. One important distinction was that between dismissal and simple non-reappointment, at least one college referring to the former when it meant the latter. Another distinction which seemed important, but which was almost never made, was that between dismissal and forced resignation. From the point of view of the main purpose and result, there may be no difference between these two types of separation; from the point of view of the right to "due process," however, the distinction is significant. The fact that the safeguards of fairness in dismissal proceedings (Items 6-*b* through 6-*g*) are almost never used, because dismissals almost never occur, may appear to make them superfluous. Their very existence, however, may fortify the position of the faculty member who is being judged, thus assuring that if forced resignation does occur, it does so by the choice of the individual, as a preferred alternative to formal dismissal proceedings.

ITEM 6-A. *Processes designed to assure fairness in decision of non-reappointment.*—Only two colleges—Sarah Lawrence and Vassar—have formal guarantees to assure full and fair consideration

37

of a faculty member's case before the decision not to reappoint is made. Several of the others have less formal understandings that any faculty member can take his case to the president or to the appropriate faculty judicial body. The operation of these provisions could not be examined, of course, from the point of view which might be most pertinent, that of ex-appointees, who, having left the institution, were not on hand for interviews.

ITEMS 6-B THROUGH 6-F. *Provisions relating to grounds for dismissal, formal statement of charges, formal hearing, appeal or further hearing, and final legal action required.*—With respect to the dismissal of faculty members, seven colleges have prescribed procedures that seem to be in accord with the AAUP–AAC *Principles.* Wesleyan had no provisions of this sort, other than the requirement of "due notice and investigation," until the spring of 1953, when conditions outside the university focused attention on the need for advance agreement about the handling of cases of alleged subversive connections of faculty members. Swarthmore represents the atypical situation, having no written provisions except the guarantee of a statement of reasons for dismissal (or for "demotion"—the only reference to demotion in the eight colleges). The writer received the impression, however, that Swarthmore was no less committed to fair processes than the other seven institutions.

The composition of the body before whom the accused teacher is given a hearing is presumably an important factor in the justice of the process. Of the seven institutions that have a prescribed hearing process, four assign the hearing to a faculty committee and three to a joint trustee-faculty group. Three of the four faculty committees are the regular elected standing advisory committees of their respective faculties, while the fourth is a specially designated group. Only two institutions have a written provision for an appeal and a second hearing. Vassar provides for a second hearing before the trustee Committee on Faculty and Studies, and Hobart provides for one by the governing board itself. Dismissal contrary to the recommendation resulting from the first hearing requires a two-thirds vote of the board at Hobart, and at Vassar the second committee may not reverse the recommendation of

38

the first without affording opportunity for conference with the latter.

There are wide variations in the prescribed details of the hearing process. Numerous features of the AAUP–AAC *Principles*, such as those that concern the providing of counsel, the admission of evidence, and the keeping of a stenographic record, are missing in most of the eight colleges (see Comparative Synopsis, pp. 142–144). The extent to which their procedures approximate those of the AAUP–AAC *Principles* could be discussed at length, but since there is seldom occasion to invoke this machinery, it would be unrealistically speculative to devote considerable discussion here to the comparative merits of details of procedure. Indeed, no illustration of the actual operation of formal provisions now existing was forthcoming from any of the eight institutions.

ITEM 6-G. *Guarantee of an equitable salary settlement in case of dismissal.*—Four institutions have legislation governing salary settlement in case of dismissal, and one other is understood to subscribe to AAUP–AAC *Principles* in the matter. Since, however, involuntary separation of faculty members with tenure or unexpired term appointments is almost never brought about by formal dismissal, the salary settlement in all but the rarest cases would not be governed by the regulations concerning dismissal. In each case recalled by the officers consulted, the college involved had either paid the contract amount in full or, in the case of a continuous appointment, a semester's salary.

SALARY POLICY

Principle 7: The right to be governed by a salary policy that is understood, consistent, and determined in the light of consultation with those affected by it

ITEMS 7-A THROUGH 7-C. *Existence of a published scale; faculty participation in the shaping of salary policy; guarantee of conformity to scale.*—The subject of salary policies was so frequently a controversial one that it will be considered in detail in the case studies of individual colleges in the following chapter. Certain generalizations, however, may be made here. In the three

39

colleges where the salary scale was either nonexistent or unpublished there was criticism of this fact, and apparently it was a source of some insecurity. The criticisms ranged, in intensity, from the charge that secretiveness was designed to conceal inequities to the suggestion that, although treatment was probably as favorable without a published scale as with one, it would be reassuring to know what the scale was.

Only Vassar has a written commitment that individual salaries must conform to the official scale, and some of the colleges do not recognize this principle as desirable. The Colgate salary scale consists of minimum figures only, and there is overlapping between ranks, as there is in the official scale at Hobart. The scales at Haverford, Vassar, and Wesleyan do not have overlapping between ranks. The administration of faculty salaries at Sarah Lawrence, which is unique among the colleges studied, was discussed in connection with Item 3-*b* and will be taken up again in the case study of that institution in Chapter III.

Participation of the faculty in the formulation of salary policy varies widely. In several colleges there is considerable unsolicited advisory activity by the local chapter of the American Association of University Professors, while in others there are joint trustee-faculty committee consultations formalized by statute.

INSURANCE AND EMPLOYEE BENEFITS

Principle 8: The right to such assistance in matters of personal and family responsibility as the institution is in a position to provide, and the obligation to avail oneself of such help as may forestall one's ever becoming an economic liability, moral or legal, of the institution

The provisions that might be included under this principle are numerous, and it was not the writer's purpose to make a complete summary or analysis of them. His interest was in the extent to which there was written or otherwise formal recognition of faculty rights and obligations in this area.

ITEM 8-A. *Privileges and obligations in matters of housing.*— College-owned housing for faculty members is usually administered by the president's office, priorities being determined by some single criterion, such as date of application. In several colleges, notably Haverford, Mount Holyoke, and Vassar, there are extensive provisions defining housing policies, including the terms of the landlord-tenant relationship.

Other housing privileges, such as the right to build on college land, the right to continue occupancy of college dwellings after retirement, the right of the family of a deceased faculty member to continue occupancy for a time, and the availability of building loans at low interest rates, are encountered occasionally, and these privileges are sometimes formalized in trustee legislation. All institutions appear to provide much informal "house-hunting" assistance for members who cannot enjoy the privileges of college-owned housing.

Housing is occasionally a controversial subject, and in several of the eight colleges faculty committees have been consulted by the administration or board, or both, in formulating housing policies. Such consultation is a statutory requirement at Vassar.

ITEM 8-B. *Optional and required participation in insurance, retirement, and other plans to meet personal risks.*—Seven of the eight institutions have life insurance or term insurance plans, three of which are paid for partly or wholly by the college. Participation is compulsory in several institutions. At Colgate, for example, the insurance is expressly intended "to help protect the families of the younger members of the Faculty, while the TIAA retirement account is being built up."[6] The regulation requires that the faculty member either take out the insurance sponsored by the university or present satisfactory evidence of carrying equivalent insurance.

The life insurance policy sponsored by Vassar, of which the college pays for the first one thousand dollars, is of interest because of the requirement that the beneficiary "be so designated that the insurance shall be available for expenses in case of the death of the insured while in service."[7] Both the Colgate and the Vassar provisions mentioned here seem to imply that the indi-

[6] *Faculty Handbook,* p. 13.
[7] *Academic Statute,* Art. X, sec. 10A, in *Governance of Vassar College.*

41

vidual has an obligation to provide against becoming a liability of the institution. It was pointed out to the writer by one administrative officer that since the college could not stand by without providing some assistance in the event of personal or family tragedy, it behooved the school and the faculty member to make such advance provision as seemed practicable.

All eight colleges have pension plans through the Teachers Insurance and Annuity Association of America, and most of them either have or are considering the added feature of membership in the College Retirement Equities Fund. Four have compulsory participation after a certain number of years of service, qualifications and exceptions being made in each college. Mount Holyoke's rule is unique in that, while requiring participation in a pension plan, it allows a choice between TIAA and any one of a number of commercial plans satisfactory to the college. The plan at Vassar is unique in that the college has recently assumed the entire cost of TIAA participation, the contribution being 15 per cent.

ITEM 8-C. *An objectively determined time of retirement.*—All eight colleges have specifically stated ages for retirement, either in codified legislation or in information bulletins. Three specify a different age for voluntary and compulsory retirement; and five, either by written policy or by understood practice, reserve the option of the trustees to postpone retirement. The trustees of Vassar reserve the right to retire a faculty member at any time for reasons of health, while guaranteeing him the right of medical examination by a physician chosen by agreement between the faculty member and the college.

ITEM 8-D. *Miscellaneous other privileges.*—Although the writer attempted to gather comparative data on all the most significant aspects of faculty rights and obligations, it is conceivable that items worthy of notice may have been overlooked. In order to present in the Comparative Synopsis practices that, while not examined in all eight colleges, may be of general interest, the item "Miscellaneous other privileges" has been included.

One such right or privilege is the assistance given to faculty members in providing for educational opportunities for their

42

own children. Tuition exchange plans and tuition-waiving plans were found frequently and were said to be on the increase. These were not always stated in any published document but were based, at least in most colleges, on a formal act of the governing board. Other privileges, such as sick leave, seldom received written formalization, and inquiry regarding them led to the conclusion that the trustees were often considerably more liberal than they could prudently commit themselves in advance to be. Cases were reported, in colleges having no written policy on sick leave, in which full salary had been paid for most or all of a year, when no services had been rendered during that time. No feeling was expressed in favor of further formalization of sick leave privileges than that which already existed.

ACADEMIC FREEDOM

Principle 9: The right to encouragement and protection in the activities appropriate to a member of a professional body dedicated to the search for and dissemination of truth, and the obligations associated with this right[8]

ITEM 9-A. *Guarantees relating to academic freedom in general.*— Four colleges have trustee legislation guaranteeing academic freedom as interpreted by them, and a fifth, Sarah Lawrence, has a policy statement by the trustees that might be considered a formal commitment to principles. Hobart, while not having a published commitment on this matter, formulated a general statement of principles for submission to the Commission on Institutions of Higher Education of the Middle States Association of Colleges and Secondary Schools, in connection with the 1953 re-evaluation of the college. All eight institutions seem to endorse the AAUP–AAC *Principles* in the matter of academic freedom, whether or not they have formally adopted them.

---

[8] No presumption is made as to what the precise activities are in which the faculty member has a right to be protected. The literature on academic freedom, however, clearly suggests that there are rights and obligations necessary to the performance of the academic profession's distinctive functions. Principle 9 and the applications of it that have been included in the Academic Bill of Rights and Obligations represent the writer's expression of this view as reflected in these and other institutions.

43

While there were occasional reservations expressed as to the completeness of academic freedom that existed on these eight campuses, there were no serious charges, and the writer is not inclined to try to relate the quality of academic freedom existing to the presence or absence of formal policies on the subject. The eight colleges studied have relatively long liberal traditions, and every one has in its history evidence of belief in a strong, free faculty.[9] One would not expect to find in these colleges examples of gross abuse of governing and administrative powers to stifle the processes of free discussion and criticism or to cripple other personal freedoms. No such abuse was remembered in recent times, if at all, by the persons interviewed.

A feeling occasionally implied and at least once explicitly expressed was that academic freedom was a relative condition only. While no person on the faculty at the present time, it was said, held views so radical as to embarrass the authorities of the college, considerable pressure would probably be brought to bear on any faculty member whose utterances seemed to challenge the basic tenets held by people of influence in college affairs. It was also pointed out, occasionally with approval, that like-mindedness with the present college community was a factor in the selection of new faculty members. At Wesleyan, an official statement of qualities to be sought in selecting new faculty members includes "suitability for the Wesleyan Community."[10] At another college, one with denominational ties, a faculty member suggested that open denial of the Trinity in the 1920's would have caused a great deal of trouble, even though the college in question was one where religious freedom was especially emphasized. "They never took in anybody here unless they liked him," another faculty member said. In a third college, a junior faculty member who was in other respects somewhat critical said that the atmosphere among members of the administration and the faculty was so harmonious that to initiate vigorous criticism within the organization would

[9] Even Sarah Lawrence, new as it is, may be said to possess a long tradition, because of the origin in Vassar of some of its conceptual framework and because of the Vassar background of its early leadership.

[10] By-Laws of the Academic Council, chap. ii, sec. 7. This phrase was not intended, of course, to limit academic freedom, and whether it could ever operate in this way is a matter of opinion.

be personally disagreeable and unrewarding, and that such behavior was perhaps subconsciously avoided on that account.

One factor operating subtly against academic freedom, of course, is the inevitable influence of personal relationships in determining appointments and promotions of faculty members. Personal likes and dislikes can easily be rationalized into arguments of competence and incompetence. It follows that, where reappointments and promotions depend on the judgment of only one person, academic freedom may be only as secure as the objectivity of that one person.

The remarks made in connection with departmental affairs (Items 14-*a* through 14-*d*) emphasize the inevitability of a degree of subjective, personal control, particularly of junior members who have not had time to win prestige outside their departments. What happens in a departmental situation can also happen in the college as a whole, especially if the faculty is as homogeneous in outlook as some of the foregoing comments suggest. Even though the right of the scholar to differ with the community at large may be accepted, the microcosm of the campus—the locus of his more intimate day-to-day contacts—may place in an uncomfortable plight the member whose views differ sharply from those of his colleagues. In fact, a politically conservative person on a politically liberal faculty may be in a situation similar to that of the political "radical" in the larger community. Such a situation can be very difficult for the junior scholar who has not yet made his mark in his field.

The comments referred to in the preceding paragraphs suggest the difficulty of regulating, by statutory action, questions of such subtle and changing aspect as academic freedom. A member of the Advisory Committee at Vassar, who enthusiastically supported the Vassar *Governance* as a useful instrument, thought it was neither necessary nor practicable to "regulate in advance," in considerable detail, such matters as academic freedom. It is significant that Vassar, which probably has the most extensive experience of any college in this group with formalization of principles, recently dropped a proposal to expand the section of the *Governance* dealing with academic freedom. This section is similar

45

in major particulars to the AAUP–AAC *Principles* and is of about the same length.

The admitted undesirability of highly detailed prescriptions concerning academic freedom, however, does not render all written regulation in this area useless; it merely emphasizes the need for flexibility. Flexibility, the writer feels, is admirably achieved by the provision[11] in the *Governance of Vassar College* that commits the trustees to discuss with the appropriate faculty body any situation involving an issue of academic freedom. The president of one of the other colleges studied mentioned to the writer that such a procedure would have saved a large university from a major trustee-faculty conflict, which drew much unfavorable publicity. If it *is* impracticable to "regulate in advance" such matters as those of academic freedom, perhaps the statutory guarantee that the important channels of communication will be kept open is the most realistic advance protection available. The question of trustee-faculty communication is discussed further in connection with Principle 16.

ITEMS 9-B THROUGH 9-D. *Qualifications and obligations relating to the guarantee of academic freedom; provisions governing outside employment; provisions governing absence from campus during academic year.*—Several colleges have explicit limitations on the teacher's freedom, sometimes stated in connection with the guarantee of academic freedom and sometimes stated elsewhere. The policies in some institutions follow closely the AAUP–AAC *Principles* regarding the teacher's obligations, while in others they are more specifically adapted to the situation of the particular college. Sarah Lawrence, for example, requires faculty members by individual contract provisions to keep campus hours for which they are appointed. The question of devoting proper time and effort to the college appointment did not appear elsewhere to be a current issue, although faculty members were said, in most colleges, to engage in a great many outside activities, both remunerative and otherwise. There seemed to be no widespread feeling that more rules were needed than already existed.

[11] *Academic Statute*, Art. VII, sec. 5B(1)e, in *Governance of Vassar College*.

46

Principle 10: The right to equal consideration with others,
regardless of creed in religious or other matters

ITEM 10-A. *Regulations regarding loyalty oaths.*—The colleges
in Massachusetts and New York require the signing of the state
loyalty oath, although Colgate is the only one with a written statement to that effect. The governing boards of both Haverford and
Swarthmore went on public record as opposing loyalty oaths.

The writer inquired at each institution concerning the effect,
on the college's pattern of academic freedom, of congressional
committees investigating allegedly subversive influences in the
colleges. The question asked was whether the problems raised
by the activities of such committees could be solved within the
framework of principles already established at the college, or
whether new principles and interpretations would have to be
formulated. In some of the colleges the trustees, or the trustees
and faculty jointly, were said to be considering the question; in
one a statement of policy had been approved by both bodies but
was not for circulation until such time as the publicity of an investigation might necessitate its release. At Colgate the president had stated in *The President's Report, 1952,* what he thought
the position of the college should be. The statement is similar in
major respects to the 1953 statement of the Association of American Universities.[12] Wesleyan has actually instituted, in advance,
a formal procedure for dealing with faculty members whose
loyalty may be placed in question by public investigations (see
Comparative Synopsis, Item 6-*d*).

The view was expressed by two senior scholars, representing
different institutions, that the principles of academic freedom
already established at their college would not and should not dis-
qualify a person for faculty membership on the basis of membership in the Communist party, but there was no indication of the
prevalence of this view.

At least two members of the eight faculties had already testified before congressional groups, and there was a feeling of ex-

[12] Association of American Universities, "The Rights and Responsibilities of
Universities and Their Faculties," *New York Times,* March 31, 1953.

pectancy on a number of campuses. At several of the colleges, as was stated before, the trustees and the faculty were working out together the principles that were to apply if the Senate investigations should involve any of them, and in at least one college the faculty had been briefed on legal aspects by a lawyer on the governing board.

ITEM 10-B. *Guarantee of religious freedom and equality.*—The charters of Hobart and Wesleyan contain provisions designed to guarantee freedom of conscience.[13] These articles, both of which are over one hundred years old, may be of historic rather than of current significance, in view of the religiously heterodox composition of most faculties and student bodies of today and the obvious assumption, on all eight campuses, that religious freedom is everyone's right. There was expressed, nevertheless, some feeling that treatment of individuals in matters of promotion and salary increase was not always unmindful of religious affiliation. This feeling was not encountered on most of the campuses, however, and it was nowhere widespread.

There seemed to be no significant difference between the concept of academic freedom held by the colleges having religious affiliations and that held by the nonsectarian group, except perhaps in point of emphasis. The internal documents of only two institutions make reference to the teacher's obligations relative to religious questions. Haverford faculty members are "expected" to attend the Quaker meetings of the college body at least occasionally, according to an administration statement. Sarah Lawrence requires that "there be no indoctrination of students with a political, philosophical, or religious dogma."[14] None of the institutions having a religious connection is under the organizational control of its denomination.

---

[13] Colgate was also at one time indirectly covered by such a provision. The Baptist Education Society, which shared in the government of the college (then Madison University) through a compact with the board of trustees, had an article in its charter providing that any action of the society that affected freedom of conscience would automatically void the charter.

[14] Statement approved by Executive Committee of the Board of Trustees, January 3, 1952, and quoted in Harold Taylor, President, and Harrison Tweed, Chairman of the Board of Trustees, "Letter to the Students, Faculty, and Alumnae Council of Sarah Lawrence College," January 18, 1952.

ASSISTANCE TOWARD PROFESSIONAL GROWTH

Principle 11: The right to assistance from the institution, through sabbatical leave or other means, in furthering one's development as a professional person, and the obligations associated with receipt of such assistance

ITEMS 11-A THROUGH 11-C. *Designation of persons who may obtain sabbatical leave; provision for equitable awarding of sabbatical leave; obligations associated with award of sabbatical leave.*—No consistent view of the principles governing sabbatical leave was found in these institutions, except that none of them formally recognizes such leave as an earned right. Several institutions do, however, define the conditions and the intent with which sabbatical leave is awarded. The most notable points of contrast in policy are given in the following paragraphs.

Four colleges have written statements relating to the granting of sabbatical leave. One of the four, Wesleyan, has merely an informative item in the Appendix of the *By-Laws of the Academic Council,* a document that follows rather than regulates practice. Vassar, another of the four mentioned above, does not recognize the term *sabbatical leave* but substitutes a system of "Faculty Fellowships," a program for fostering the professional growth of faculty members through leaves and research grants. An aspect of this program is in effect sabbatical leave, though if leave of absence is accompanied by financial compensation, the money is received as a fellowship grant, not as regular salary.

Except for Colgate and Hobart, each college in the group has a program of subsidized leave of absence that approximates the sabbatical in the usual sense. Hobart does have a provision for such leave, recorded in the minutes of the trustees, but financial resources have not always been sufficient to implement it. Swarthmore, while having no published statements on the subject, actually seems to be the most liberal in the granting of sabbatical leave.

The demand for sabbaticals varies considerably, and it was even reported in one institution that faculty members were often

49

reluctant to incur the expense of taking a leave because of their family responsibilities. One instance was reported of the forcing of sabbatical leave on a faculty member by the president.

The only official statement of obligations associated with subsidized leave is that of Vassar. A faculty fellowship, whether it involves leave of absence or not, is awarded only on the approval of a project by the college (nominally by the trustees) after its presentation to the elected faculty Committee on Research. The Vassar provision also requires a report to the Committee on Research upon the conclusion of the project.

In other colleges the obligations connected with leave subsidized by the institution are much less clear. At one college, for example, the writer encountered two views: (1) that sabbatical leave may be spent in any way the faculty member chooses; (2) that the time is to be spent in some professionally stimulating way.

In three colleges the awarding of sabbatical leave or its equivalent is a matter of the president's recommendation and the board's approval, no faculty consultation being required. Both at Sarah Lawrence and at Vassar the award is determined primarily by a committee representing the faculty. At Mount Holyoke the recommendation of the department seems to be the important step prior to action by the president.

ITEMS 11-D AND 11-E. *Provisions for travel allowance and other assistance in efforts toward professional growth.*—All eight colleges grant travel allowance for attendance at professional meetings, the funds being administered by a faculty committee at Swarthmore, by the departments at Mount Holyoke, by the divisions at Colgate, by the administration in consultation with the departments at Hobart, and on a statutory formula at Vassar. Various arrangements exist for the handling of other funds for assistance to faculty members, depending on the amounts available for such purposes. The most extensive provisions are those of Vassar, which will be discussed further in the section on Vassar in Chapter III.

The writer did not inquire systematically concerning unwritten but accepted policies for assisting professional endeavors through

50

reduced teaching programs, clerical and typing aid, and publication aid; and no information of special significance emerged concerning these practices. Several institutions have faculty committees for the purpose of helping members obtain foundation grants. A number of presidents are personally active in these efforts, in behalf of individual colleagues as well as their institutions.

ADDITIONAL RESPONSIBILITIES
TO INSTITUTION AND TO STUDENTS

Principle 12: The obligation to exercise one's professional freedom within the limits of service to the educational enterprise of which one is a member

ITEMS 12-A AND 12-B. *Provisions governing adherence to academic schedule and maintenance of academic standards and purposes.*—Principle 12 is not expressed as a complete proposition in any of the documents studied, though considerable written regulation exists that seems to express a recognition of the teacher's obligations to the educational enterprise he serves. Rules regarding faculty members' responsibilities in two areas, academic schedule and academic standards, were selected as among the more important kinds of provisions to compare. One college allows no canceling or postponing of academic engagements without administrative approval; five others permit various degrees of freedom in the matter; and two institutions make no mention of the subject.

The obligation to observe the academic standards and accepted purposes of the organization as a whole is expressed in a number of statements requiring the teacher to relate his grading of students' work to understood distribution patterns. Neither at Mount Holyoke nor at Swarthmore, where such statements appear in written rules, are individual faculty members ever officially asked to take action in observance of the requirement. The extent to which this really is an officially recognized obligation of the teacher would seem to depend entirely on whether there is active machinery working to correct discrepancies, as there is at Vassar.

51

*Principle 13: The obligation to observe duly
the rights and responsibilities of students*

ITEMS 13-A THROUGH 13-C. *Provisions relating to evaluation of
students' work, handling of academic dishonesty cases, and helping of individual students.*—Obligations toward students, only
selected aspects of which could be examined in this study, are
recognized in a variety of written and unwritten provisions in
each college. In most of the colleges the student body has some
responsibility, even if only consultative, in academic affairs; and
in several, joint student-faculty committees operate in a number
of areas.[15] The responsibilities of the individual faculty member
in each situation vary with the number of committee assignments
he holds relating to student matters.

The three areas selected for inclusion in the Academic Bill of
Rights and Obligations are perhaps more closely related to the
rights and obligations of students than to those of faculty members, though certain points are worth mentioning here. Mount
Holyoke limits the teacher's authority to drop a student from a
course, requiring action by a faculty committee in order to assure justice to the student. Academic dishonesty cases may be
handled at the teacher's discretion in two colleges, though those
that have formal provisions on the subject require that a central
record be kept of such incidents. In other colleges a faculty or
a joint student-faculty committee handles the matter, up to the
point of disciplinary measures; and in some a student-operated
honor system performs both investigating and, to a limited extent,
disciplinary functions in cases of alleged academic dishonesty by
students.

The most specific formal obligation to help individual students
is that found at Sarah Lawrence, where the advisory system provides the basis of continuity in each student's program. This advisory work is part of the teacher's instructional load and an

[15] The grant of power from the faculty to the student body, and the student
government documents based on that grant, were among the most legalistic
documents encountered in several of the colleges studied. At Mount Holyoke
and Vassar the authority of the student government rests on a formal grant from
the faculty, which, in turn, is based on codified enabling legislation of the trustees.

understood part of his contractual commitment upon appointment to the faculty.

RELATIONSHIP TO DEPARTMENT

Principle 14: The right to work in a departmental
or divisional unit that is reasonably free from
the arbitrary domination of an individual or a limited group

ITEMS 14-A THROUGH 14-D. *Manner of selection and term of tenure of department chairman; participation of department members in decisions on appointments and promotions and in other affairs of the department; provisions designed to assure equitable distribution of teaching load.*—Departmental administration is not a subject of considerable legislation except in the two most formally governed colleges. In these institutions, as well as in the other five that are organized along departmental lines, the impression formed was that the extent of democracy in a departmental situation was dependent primarily on personal factors.

The faculty member's dependence on the support of the department chairman in matters of appointment and promotion is perhaps such a strong consideration in setting the pattern of relationships that rules for democratic operation mean little. Both in colleges that have elected advisory groups on appointments and in those that do not, it was often said that the administration was very reluctant to override a department chairman. There was some feeling, among junior faculty members in colleges where department chairmen are appointed for an indefinite period of time, that chairmen should be elected or that the office should be rotated. This comment was no more frequent, however, than the statement that it was futile to try to legislate democratic behavior, particularly in a departmental unit. It is also futile, of course, to discuss the merits of rotating the chairmanship in departments having a membership of three, which was the median size in one of the institutions studied. For certain purposes of administration, it might well be questioned whether an organization having as its prime components the traditional subject-matter departmental units is actually suitable for small institutions.

53

RELATIONSHIP TO GENERAL FACULTY
AND ADMINISTRATION

Principle 15: The right and the obligation to play a responsible role in the over-all functions appropriate to a college faculty

ITEM 15-A. *Definition of the responsibility and the authority of the faculty as a whole.*—In five of the eight colleges the authority and the responsibility of the faculty are referred to in codified legislation of the governing board, but in only one, Vassar, is the delegation of authority sufficiently unrestricted to assure the faculty a free hand in matters assigned to it. Two of the five institutions make the authority of the faculty explicitly subject to that of the president, and two others make it explicitly subject to approval by the board. The three institutions in which faculty authority is not defined, however, seem to operate with a clear idea of what it is, and the impression was conveyed to the writer that this authority was thoroughly respected by the trustees. The following comments illustrate this point: "Our security is in the fact that we actually run things" (Sarah Lawrence); "It is inconceivable that the board would ever reverse a faculty action" (Swarthmore).

The drawing up of the documents of government to allow the faculty its full scope of responsibility while preserving the board's freedom to discharge its own responsibility has caused some concern in at least two institutions because of the overlapping of areas of trustee and faculty interests. Mount Holyoke and Vassar recognize this problem by designating the overlapping areas and requiring trustee-faculty conference on any question arising therein. One institution that did not grant its faculty an area of final responsibility recently suffered the embarrassment of having an important program change questioned by the board several months after the faculty had executed it. The institution in question is not one of those with regularized conference procedures.

ITEMS 15-B AND 15-C. *Definition of faculty membership and of voting rights.*—No two of the six institutions that define faculty membership have the same criteria for it. Certain administrative

54

officers in addition to the president are counted as faculty members in most cases, though not even the head librarian is always included. Those whose rank is below that of instructor; part-time teachers; and teachers in special classifications, such as lecturers, are considered faculty members in some colleges but not in others. Apart from a certain measure of social or professional prestige presumably conferred, the exact significance of faculty membership is difficult to determine, since not all faculty members are allowed to vote in all faculty actions. Furthermore, voting rights in faculty meeting are sometimes possessed by persons who are not, by definition, faculty members.

Faculty voting rights present a picture no more uniform than faculty membership. Several institutions stipulate a period of time that must be served by new instructors, usually one or two years, before they may vote; and there are sometimes other qualifications as well. At Vassar there are two separate classes of suffrage in faculty meetings, one for educational matters and one for general matters. In only three colleges are voting rights prescribed by published rule; in two of these—Colgate and Mount Holyoke—the question of who shall vote is covered in the by-laws of the trustees; in the third—Vassar—suffrage is a jurisdiction formally delegated to the faculty by the governing board.

ITEMS 15-D THROUGH 15-H. *Frequency of faculty meetings; rights of participation in faculty meetings; composition of important policy-making committees; access to such committees by faculty members.*—In addition to differences in the matter of voting rights, there was wide variation in the extent of official recognition given to the faculty member's right and obligation to share responsibly in the direction of the whole educational enterprise. One extreme position is represented by the provisions for elaborate parliamentary machinery contained in the Vassar *Governance;* the other is represented by the total absence of such provisions at Swarthmore. The other institutions occupy intermediate positions between these two, with respect both to the number of standing committees and to the number of written regulations relating to their operation.

Taking the eight colleges together, probably no area of faculty rights and obligations revealed a greater divergence of opinion on the value of written prescription than did this one. To some people a highly articulate written constitution represented a beacon of understanding and a bulwark of security, while to others it represented a picayune misdirection of effort. The specific arguments on this matter are set forth in Chapter IV.

RELATIONSHIP TO GOVERNING BOARD

Principle 16: The right to a direct means of communication with the governing board of the institution

ITEM 16-A. *Provisions for faculty conference with, or representation on, the governing board.*—The extent to which direct trustee-faculty communication is a recognized principle is presumed to be pertinent to the topic of faculty rights and obligations, in view of the fact that some institutions do regard it as a right. The availability of unofficial channels of communication, of course, might be of more value to an individual than the guarantee of an official one, and in this connection it is important whether a substantial number of the active trustees reside where they tend to be accessible to faculty members on a social basis, as is true in the case of Haverford, or whether they reside at a considerable distance, as in the case of several other institutions. Despite the possible effectiveness of casual contacts for some purposes, however, much thought has been given in some institutions to the maintenance of regular, official channels.

Two institutions have effective faculty representation on the board of trustees, and the subject of representation is under trustee-faculty discussion in a third, Mount Holyoke. At Sarah Lawrence the representation is clearly legal, since the charter authorizes the board of trustees to choose its members and the by-laws of the trustees call for nomination by the teaching faculty of one of the candidates to be elected by the board. At Haverford, as is discussed in greater detail later, the representation is not legalized (see pp. 90–91).

Conference between trustees and faculty occurs in at least some areas in all the colleges. Recognition of this practice varies;

at Mount Holyoke and Vassar it is a statutory obligation of both bodies, while at Sarah Lawrence it is an option of the faculty, guaranteed by statute. The functional scope of the practice ranges from general communication, as at Hobart, to special-purpose communication only, as at Colgate. The procedure ranges in regularity from a routine requirement, as at Hobart and Mount Holyoke, to an optional but frequent practice, as in the informal visiting program at Wesleyan. Arrangements vary in permanence from standing machinery, as at Hobart and several other colleges, to an *ad hoc* procedure, as at Swarthmore. In several colleges the conference relationship between the faculty and the trustees seems to be the organizational feature that gives the greatest satisfaction to the faculty. Perhaps the most succinct statement of the advantages of trustee-faculty conference arrangements was offered by a member of the Haverford faculty who had served on a number of joint committees and was also a faculty representative on the board of trustees. Every activity that brings groups into contact with each other, he said, makes it more difficult for them to treat each other as stereotypes.

ITEM 16-B. *Provisions for faculty participation in the choice of principal officers of the institution.*—None of the colleges has written provisions specifically relating to the role of the faculty in selecting the president, though several faculties have been consulted by their trustees as a matter of course, and at least one faculty in the group offered its trustees unsolicited help. Several of the current presidencies seem to have been filled largely on faculty advice. It is unlikely that in any of these colleges the trustees would, under current conditions, fail to seek faculty opinion in choosing a president. The role of the faculty in the selection of other officers is officially prescribed in several institutions.

CHAPTER III

STUDIES OF
SELECTED COLLEGES

Introduction

In addition to the investigation of specific practices on a comparative basis throughout the eight colleges, a study was made of each institution as a unique whole, presenting a pattern of faculty rights and obligations peculiar to its own situation. This "case study" approach seemed necessary if the various provisions were to be understood in their proper context. Four of the eight studies are presented in this chapter as representative of the contrasting types of patterns found. The order in which they are arranged is one of progression from the most formal pattern to the least formal, and in the complete report of the study the grouping was as follows: most formal—Vassar College, Mount Holyoke College; less formal—Colgate University, Sarah Lawrence College, Wesleyan University; least formal—Hobart College, Haverford College, Swarthmore College.

This classification is not valid for all the subjects with which the study is concerned, for one college may have many written rules in one area of rights and obligations and very few in another, while in a sister institution the reverse may be true. For example, the grouping of Colgate University with Sarah Lawrence College and Wesleyan University is not intended to imply the existence of specific similarities between Colgate and either of the two latter institutions. The reason for this grouping is that, while the documents bearing upon rights and obligations of faculty members are in general less extensive and less prescriptive in these three institutions than at Vassar or Mount Holyoke, rights and obligations are more carefully set down in writing than at Hobart or Swarthmore. The similarity of the colleges in this middle group, however, hardly goes beyond this rough quantitative measure.

The Sarah Lawrence documents prescribe the constitution and functions of faculty machinery in all areas, including those of appointments and salaries, whereas Colgate has no formal faculty participation in these matters. Colgate has detailed statutory guarantees relating to academic freedom and tenure, while Sarah Lawrence has no clear statutory provisions in either area, and only a general public statement regarding academic freedom. Wesleyan does have a faculty committee, governed by rather precisely prescribed procedures, on matters of appointment, but its members are elected by professors and not by the full faculty. And in the area of tenure, Wesleyan has no body of written principles. Hence the classification that has been accorded these three institutions should be taken only as a starting point for discussion, and not as a major proposition to be established by further examination.

VASSAR COLLEGE

General description

Of all the institutions studied, Vassar College has the most highly organized and detailed body of written doctrine concerning the rights and obligations of faculty members. The documents embodying the principles by which the college is governed are the result of efforts toward improved codification on the part of trustees, administration, and faculty over a period of thirty years. Important features of the Vassar pattern have counterparts in other institutions considered in this book, but none of the others has both the comprehensive coverage and the systematic and explicit relating of rights and obligations to their several authoritative sources. A standing committee of the faculty is assigned the responsibility of codifying faculty actions. Besides the Committee on Faculty Procedure, as it is called, special committees have on occasion been set up to prepare major revisions of the governing documents for action by the trustees and the faculty, according to their respective areas of jurisdiction.

The Vassar documents, only limited parts of which are strictly relevant to this study, fill a seventy-page issue of the college *Bulletin*, entitled *Governance of Vassar College*. The *Governance*, as it is referred to on the campus, contains the college charter, together with amendments in effect; currently effective legislation by the trustees; and legislation passed by the faculty on authority delegated by the trustees. The section immediately following the charter and amendments is entitled *By-Laws of the Board of Trustees*. Then comes a brief section entitled *Principles Underlying Relations of Trustees and Faculty*, and, finally, the *Academic Statute*. The *By-Laws* and *Principles* are documents of the board exclusively, but the *Statute* contains both legislation by the board and legislation by the faculty on the authority conferred by the board in the *Principles* section.

The charter contains only one item especially pertinent to the topic of this study, the stipulation that "no president or professor of the college shall be appointed or removed, except by the affirmative vote of a majority of all the Trustees."[1] The *By-Laws*, as those of most other colleges in the study, deal with the powers, organization, and procedures of the board and with the business affairs of the corporation. The matters covered in the *By-Laws* are of concern to this study only as they specify the work of the board committees that deal with the faculty.

The next section, *Principles Underlying Relations of Trustees and Faculty*, states the principles of academic freedom, defines the area of authority delegated to the faculty, and specifies the basis of individual faculty members' contracts. The concept of academic freedom it expresses is similar to that which is embodied

[1] *Governance of Vassar College*, Pt. II, sec. 6.

60

n the AAUP–AAC *Principles.* This section of the *Governance* also delegates to the faculty responsibility for educational policy, with the reservation that policies in certain areas, notably those involving "substantial change in the character of academic degrees or considerable financial adjustment," are to be the subject of trustee-faculty conference.[2] A number of other faculty jurisdictions, such as the library, are also specified in this section. The principle of conference between trustees and faculty is explicitly recognized, and the conditions and procedures for such conference are set forth. The requirement of a contract as "the sole basis of the individual's service in the college" is also included in this section, and the contents of individual contracts are broadly specified.

The *Academic Statute* is the most extensive section of the *Governance.* It prescribes the powers and duties of the principal officers of the college, the organization and procedures of the faculty and its component parts, and the terms of service of individual faculty members. Since the *Statute* includes regulations of both the trustees and the faculty, each provision is marked with a symbol to indicate the promulgating authority. The respective areas of legislative jurisdiction of the board and the faculty are more carefully drawn at Vassar than at any other institution studied. Certain parts of the *Statute* may be changed by a vote of the faculty only, while others require action of the trustees, although much, if not most, legislation of the latter class originated with the faculty.

Development of the Vassar pattern

The development of the main body of documents of government at Vassar dates from about 1921, which saw the beginning of a joint effort by members of the faculty, trustees, and alumni, together with President Henry Noble MacCracken, to study problems of organization and relationships throughout the institution and to formulate governing principles. "Much constitutional thinking," in the words of Dr. MacCracken, was done by this group during the period from 1921 to 1923. Some of the impor-

2 *Governance of Vassar College,* Pt. IV, Art. II, sec. 1.

tant principles now embodied in the *Governance* were first adopted then, the principle of conference between trustees and faculty being an example. The *By-Laws* were first adopted in 1922, and the *Statute* in 1923. The present *Governance* has evolved from numerous revisions of these component documents.

The impression conveyed by the various faculty members interviewed was that, in general, these governing documents have been developed in an orderly, friendly way. Periods of strained relationships were said to have been occasioned more often by splits within the faculty than by differences between the faculty and the administration or the trustees. Uneasiness in feelings, it was said, has never reached the point of open hostility, and the resolution of difficulties has tended to increase the stature of the *Governance* as a constitutional, stabilizing force.

The most recent revision of the *Statute* and the *Principles* was adopted by the trustees in 1951 after many months of work by a special faculty committee, with the participation of the faculty as a whole and of the trustees. There is constant modification of the provisions contained in these sections by the trustees and the faculty, and the need for a further general revision has already been mentioned. The Committee on Faculty Procedure is attempting to devise a means of systematizing, for the record, both the formal actions taken by the faculty and the thinking that has taken place on every issue, even when no formal action has resulted.

The provisions contained in the *Governance* have come to be adopted in a variety of ways, some having developed from practice and others having been deliberately conceived in an effort to remedy some difficulty. An example of the latter is the provision that the Advisory Committee must consider at least once every five years the promotion of associate professors at maximum salary for their rank and the salary advancement of full professors not at maximum salary. This provision was a deliberate invention to eliminate the injustice that was felt to result on occasion when faculty members had achieved continuous tenure and there was no longer any required procedure to assure that their merits would be properly appraised and rewarded.

Specific features of the pattern

All the principles postulated in the Academic Bill of Rights and Obligations seem to be officially recognized at Vassar. Elected committees are provided to assure fair processes in matters affecting the security and opportunity of the individual, the most important of these being the powerful Advisory Committee. This committee is consulted by the president on matters of appointment, promotion, separation, and salary policy. Within the statutory framework established in these personnel areas, chiefly by the *Statute*, the Advisory Committee is a policy-making group.

Other committees whose areas of jurisdiction especially affect individual rights and obligations include the Committee on Research, whose recommendations largely determine the awarding of research grants and paid leaves of absence, and a number of other elected groups. The trustee-faculty conference arrangements should also be mentioned as protective machinery, since the outcomes of these conferences include policies on salaries, pensions, housing, and other matters of vital importance to individual faculty members. Certain trustee-faculty conference groups operate in special areas, and the general Committee on Conference with the Trustees is designated to deal with matters not specifically assigned to other joint committees.

In addition to the provision of these and other devices for promoting fairness and effective communication, specific procedures are prescribed in various parts of the *Governance* to further assure this end. Many of these are also required or at least carried out at other institutions, but a significant number of them appear only at Vassar. Mention of a few of the procedures found only at Vassar will help to demonstrate how thorough has been the effort to reduce to formal statements the principles this institution recognizes. The provision for a periodic review of each faculty member's status, which was found only at Vassar, has already been mentioned. Others are described below.

Notification to faculty member of his future prospects.—Instructional departments are required to inform each of their members of his prospects for retention or promotion in the final year of the

63

term in which he reaches maximum salary for his rank (if an instructor or assistant professor) or in the final year of his second term of appointment (if an associate professor), instead of making him wait for formal notice of termination of appointment from the administration. The time of year at which this communication is required is, however, not specified.

Protection against ill-considered or unilateral action against an appointee.[3]—The trustees may not terminate a faculty member's service without consulting the Advisory Committee and the department concerned. If the department fails to recommend reappointment, the teacher may appeal for a review of the reasons.

Changes in salary policy.—Any change in the salary scale, other than upward adjustments, must be preceded by consultation of the president with an elected faculty committee.

Initiative and participation in faculty affairs.—Although not all the following guarantees are found only at Vassar, no other college in the group has all of them. Various provisions in the *Governance* guarantee the individual's right to a voice in faculty and departmental affairs, including the right to participate in discussions and to make suggestions, the right to be consulted on the departmental budget, the right to call a meeting by petition of a certain minimum number of members, the right to lodge formal complaints, and the right to consult certain individuals and groups in authority without going through formal channels.

Academic freedom was perhaps the area in which it became most evident that the *Governance* itself is only an aspect of the pattern of understanding that prevails at Vassar, for the relatively brief written statement it contains is backed by what appears to be general confidence in the college's interpretation of it. A member of the Advisory Committee expressed the view that it was impossible to state in advance the principles of academic freedom with sufficient clarity and detail to meet all cases that might arise.

The question of amplifying the section on academic freedom

---

[3] Although the specific provisions under this heading are found only at Vassar, Sarah Lawrence does have procedures similar in intent (see p. 85; also Comparative Synopsis, Item 6-*a*).

was considered during the current revision of the *Governance,* but the proposed change was dropped by the faculty committee concerned. This fact would seem to support the view cited above and to indicate the faculty's confidence in the college's regard for academic freedom. No person whom the writer met could recall a violation of this freedom at Vassar. Pressures are felt, to be sure—for example, from parents. The administration handles these matters as problems in college relations or turns them over to the faculty directly, depending on the particular incident.

In connection with departmental recommendations on appointments and promotions, a departmental vote is called for by the *Governance,* each member below the rank of professor being allowed to vote on the case of any colleague of lower rank than himself. The departments do not generally hold an actual ballot, being small and informal; consensus, however, is said to be achieved. In the matter of new appointments, most of the departments have extensive internal discussion and cooperative action in quest of desirable candidates; much communication is also carried on with the president and the Advisory Committee in advance of formal recommendations. These procedures are extrastatutory.

In matters of departmental policy in general, including the formulation of budget recommendations, the *Governance* requires consultation by the chairman with other members. Comments on the operation of departments suggested that, as a rule, each individual has his say, but that the manner in which departments are run cannot be ascribed to the provisions in the *Governance,* for legislation as such is not very effective in this area. Some felt that the tendency toward autocratic administration was greatest in small departments, where there were only one or two senior members. Others, however, pointed out that the same situation could exist in large departments as well and that the personalities and backgrounds of the senior members were the most important factors.

The writer asked whether faculty members who felt their views were not given fair consideration often availed themselves of their statutory prerogatives of consulting the Advisory Committee,

65

instituting formal action, or otherwise by-passing their departments. It was said that faculty members were reluctant to exercise these rights, even though they were explicitly guaranteed, and seldom did so. It was pointed out, however, that the faculty as a whole showed a real readiness to hear the views of junior members. Although some of the younger teachers admitted that the committees holding the most power were manned by senior people, they felt that these committeemen had been selected in an appropriate manner and that they were truly representative of the faculty as far as their particular functions were concerned. There is a wholesome respect for the value of experience, and there seems to be no general tendency for a rift to develop between junior and senior members. When the faculty does divide on any issue, it was pointed out, the split is seldom, if ever, along seniority lines.

This picture of the faculty as a group relatively devoid of permanent blocs should not be left without mention of some bitterness, which has developed over the question of who is classified as a faculty member for purposes of academic suffrage. The faculty is now considered to include all members of the departments of instruction, and this definition is construed to exclude the staffs of the library and the department of health, as well as certain officers of student personnel administration. When the present suffrage rules were recently incorporated in the *Governance*, they were made nonretroactive for individuals possessing academic suffrage at that time. The removal of recognition from their offices, however, has been taken unwillingly by those affected. Since the faculty determines its *own* basis of suffrage, as provided for in the *Governance*, a majority can properly disfranchise a minority, and that is precisely what happened. Such a situation could not occur at Colgate, where faculty franchise is defined in the *By-Laws of the Board of Trustees*.

One other area of faculty rights and obligations to be discussed is that of assistance to the teacher in his professional development. The program of leaves, research grants, and related aids is in effect administered by the (largely elected) Committee on Research. The policies that guide the Committee are explicitly

66

embodied in the *Governance,* and may be said to emphasize the following principles: (1) The college considers itself to have a legitimate interest in what a faculty member does on his professional leave of absence. (2) The college wishes to do its share financially to help the individual do what is expected of him. (3) The determinants in the award of faculty fellowships (the term *sabbatical leave* is no longer used) are equitableness and the value of the award in terms of promise to the college, rather than compensation for exceptional service.

A faculty regulation, not yet incorporated in the *Governance,* states that the basis for a faculty fellowship is a research project acceptable to the Committee on Research. The provision further states that awards among qualifying applicants are to be made on the basis of years of service and previous leaves. The Committee is also given more discretion than the provision now in the *Governance* allows in the allocation of fellowship funds among the various ranks.

Evaluation of the Vassar pattern by faculty members

Because the pattern of faculty rights and obligations as recognized at Vassar represents clearly one of two opposing positions with respect to the subject of this study, particular attention is given at this point to the views expressed by members of the Vassar faculty regarding it. Every person interviewed at Vassar did have positive views to express on the subject of the *Governance,* whereas at several other colleges there was frequently encountered a lack of opinion about, or even interest in, the documents relating to faculty rights and obligations.

Although it was unanimously agreed that the *Governance* was an effective instrument, the reasons given for this opinion varied. It should be pointed out that each interview was more or less guided by the college officer's special area of interest and experience within the total topic, and by his readiness to offer views of his own. No effort was made to poll people systematically; hence, the incidence of a view as recorded in the following statements should not be regarded as statistical data.

Three members of the faculty offered the view that unwritten rights, though fully recognized and effective, are vulnerable in the event of a change in administration. One of these, a member of the Advisory Committee, felt that the force of tradition as a protection of rights was limited in areas of power. Trustees, it was pointed out, can be under severe pressures caused by conditions outside the college, such as an economic recession, and in a situation of this kind written commitments constitute a firmer guarantee than precedents. One faculty member felt he spoke for many colleagues, both senior and junior, when he said that the *Governance* itself was regarded as real protection rather than merely moral support.

A second value of the *Governance* was said to be its usefulness as a guide to action on the part of committees and individuals charged with carrying out particular functions on behalf of the faculty. The complexity of faculty organization and procedures makes a written guide invaluable in the consistent execution of policy by, for example, the Advisory Committee and the Committee on Research. A member of one of these committees observed that in difficult decisions between individuals or between groups of divergent interests, the existence of explicitly stated criteria, such as those embodied in the *Governance*, was a real aid to justice and consistency.

The value of an informative document in orienting new faculty members was mentioned at several institutions besides Vassar. An additional observation was made of the Vassar *Governance*, however, that seems important. It was stated that, regardless of the legal force of the statutes, there was value to individual faculty members merely in knowing that certain patterns of rights, relationships, and procedures existed. A group of teachers, for example, had felt aggrieved by some official action affecting them but had recovered their composure upon finding in the *Governance* justification for the action they had questioned.

Several faculty members felt that the Vassar document was unimportant as a functioning instrument but had considerable significance as a tangible symbol of relationships among faculty, administration, and trustees. As one professor expressed it, it is something toward which an attitude of loyalty can be fostered. Or, as a junior faculty member put it, the *Governance* serves as a kind of exhibit, a "see-what-we've-got." One teacher emphasized that the experience of working out cooperatively the principles and procedures embodied in the document was in itself of great value in promoting sound understandings and relationships among the parties concerned.

In considering adverse criticisms of the *Governance* offered by Vassar faculty members, it is necessary to distinguish those criticisms that relate especially to the topic of faculty rights and obligations and those that relate to other aspects of college government and administration. Most of the criticisms made had to do with the inflexibility of an instrument that subjects so many operations to detailed prescription. Since this inquiry is not primarily concerned with mechanics of faculty operation, such criticisms will be discussed only to the extent that they concern the rights and obligations of individuals.

A number of faculty members, including a member of the Advisory Committee, felt that conditions of tenure and separation should be more closely defined. Attention was called to cases in which involuntary separation from the faculty had been necessary for the good of the college, although no clear grounds for separation were provided in the *Governance*. The Advisory Committee and the trustees had managed to act in these cases, but it was felt that the position of the college would have been stronger if specific grounds could have been established by reference to the *Governance*. This criticism, it would appear, is more likely to be heard at a college like Vassar, where the principle of codification of rights is thoroughly established, than at a college where very few rights and obligations of individuals are codified. Where issues are regularly decided on the basis of explicit principles, the lack of explicitness is more likely to appear a lack of principle than where policies are normally understood but unwritten. Hence, as will be discussed further in Chapter IV, codification invites more codification.

Other comments disagreed with the view of the *Governance* as a type of constitution. The opinion was offered that this docu-

69

ment was primarily a committee's editing of legislation and that it lacked the formal status of a constitution. Actually, it seemed to the writer to be more than just an editing, since the contents, other than the charter, had been adopted by the trustees as a code.

One professor felt strongly that legislation should not be passed and codified on matters that were still controversial. The relatively permanent documents, he stated, should contain only fundamental principles and procedures requiring little flexibility, such as general tenets of academic freedom. Matters primarily of administrative procedure, and issues that require frequent redefining, should, he asserted, be left out. With the basic instrument as a framework, changing aspects of rights and obligations could, in his opinion, be provided for either by precedent and interpretation or by subsidiary documents having a relatively simple amendment procedure. According to this view, detailed prescriptions for electing faculty committees, for example, and policies and procedures for administering faculty housing could appropriately be set forth in subordinate documents. An example of this type of proposal already in effect is exclusion of the salary scale from the most recent revision of the *Governance*. The main policies concerning salaries were included, but the scale itself, which had been part of the 1942 revision, was omitted in 1951.

The chairman of one important committee felt that although the Vassar pattern of intrafaculty relationships was highly successful, the *Governance* was not the key to its success. Another college, she felt, would not necessarily benefit from adopting rules like those of Vassar. Even successful democratic practices such as the election of department chairmen might not be workable in another college.

The final aspect of faculty opinion considered here is the attitude toward the time-consuming and effort-consuming operations involved in carrying out the detailed provisions of the *Governance*. Most of the people questioned seemed to feel either that the sense of security gained by direct participation in the affairs of the institution was worth the cost in time or at least that the cost was not high enough to compel a change. Once it was suggested that, in reality, the multitude of detailed procedures

70

called for in the *Governance* was the price, not of having a written code of operation, but of being a faculty-run college. The formal instrument was merely reflecting faithfully the manner in which this faculty preferred to operate. The same person was conscious of a "pervasive sense of conflict and frustration" in the handling by the whole faculty of matters that could be more effectively dealt with by a faculty senate, if there were one. Apparently the right to participate in the government of the institution, as recognized at Vassar, extends even to the right to perpetuate a faculty organization that some people feel is less efficient than it need be.

Issues and trends

One matter affecting individual rights and obligations that could be described as a current issue is the granting of continuous tenure. It was noted in Chapter II that among the institutions studied, Vassar had the lowest percentage of full-time teaching faculty members with tenure (see p. 31 and Table 2). The relatively high percentage of appointees who are instructors (31 per cent) provides partial explanation of this condition. There has been a high number of retirements during the past ten years; furthermore, the faculty has increased in size during that time. The vacancies created by both of these factors have been filled largely by appointments in the junior ranks. Another circumstance contributing to a drop in the seniority of the faculty has been the development of the "House Fellow" program, which, by taking for part-time residential college duties certain junior faculty members who would otherwise be full-time teachers, has created vacancies in teaching positions. These vacancies, in turn, have been filled by new junior appointees.

The house fellow program, of course, will have a permanent effect on the seniority of the faculty, since house fellowships will presumably continue to be held by junior people. Except for this factor, however, the passage of time should gradually eliminate the difference in seniority between the Vassar faculty and the faculties of the other colleges studied, and the percentage of appointees with tenure should cease to contrast so markedly with percentages at other institutions. It should still be noted, how-

71

ever, that the tenure provisions at Vassar seem less liberal, point by point (see Comparative Synopsis, Items 4-*b* and 4-*c*), than those of most of the other colleges. A further indication of the comparative strictness of the Vassar outlook in the matter of tenure may be seen in a recent proposal to make the granting of continuous tenure to associate professors optional, instead of automatic as it is at present, upon expiration of the probationary period.[4] Although the proposal was rejected by the faculty, it is significant that it would have made Vassar the only institution in the group where an associate professor would not receive continuous tenure automatically after a probationary period.

Certain key individuals were asked what trends they could detect in the college with respect to the topic of this study. It seemed to the author that the complexity of the faculty structure and of faculty procedures must invite efforts toward simplification. It also seemed possible that echoes might have been heard at Vassar of demands in various other institutions for faculty representation on the board of trustees.

No desire for legal faculty representation on the governing board was expressed. All who were questioned felt that sufficient communication existed between faculty and board to obviate such a step. As a member of the Committee on Conference with the Trustees expressed it, the faculty has more effective representation before the trustees now than it could gain by placing one or two of its members on the board.

The question of introducing a faculty senate to reduce the time spent on many matters by the faculty as a whole has already been mentioned as arousing some interest. Even those who favored such a change, however, felt that it was unrealistic to hope for it, since the faculty was more than willing to pay the price in time and effort for its direct control of the matters under its jurisdiction. To be sure, administrative committees already handle some important faculty work according to policies laid down by the faculty. The Committee on Admissions is an example. Nevertheless, there was no opinion expressed that the

---

[4] The provision in the *Academic Statute* (Art. X, sec. 3D) now reads as follows: "Those who have served six years as associate professor at Vassar College shall receive indeterminate tenure." (See Comparative Synopsis, Item 4-*c*.)

72

extent of delegation might increase. The proposal for a senate is always voted down.

No one suggested that the quantity of codified principles and procedures might decrease, although several persons thought that some sections of the *Governance* should be less detailed. The 1951 revision of the *Governance* is approximately the same length as the 1942 revision. As already described, there has been discussion of the desirability of developing in greater detail the provisions on academic freedom. Because of the feeling that such a complex question as academic freedom cannot be closely "regulated in advance," the suggestion has not found general favor. More recently, however, the activities of congressional committees investigating allegedly subversive influences in the colleges have brought this question to the forefront, and considerable discussion among trustees, administration, and faculty has taken place concerning the precise stand of the college in the event of a faculty member's refusal to testify.

The inquiry into the Vassar pattern of faculty rights and obligations strongly suggests that faculty rights are rather fully realized and that the Vassar *Governance* plays an important part in the highly satisfactory relationships that exist. Its several values, however, might not be realizable in another institution by the introduction of a similar instrument unless this instrument came as a development consistent with the life and thought of that institution. The *Governance* has grown at Vassar along with other traditions; it was not instituted as a separate effort toward general reform.

COLGATE UNIVERSITY

General description

Colgate University has a greater number of written statements relating to the rights and obligations of faculty members than most other institutions included in this study. As will be shown presently, matters relating to conditions of appointment, such as tenure and salary, as well as professional freedoms and associated obligations, are treated in detail. To liken Colgate to Mount Holyoke and Vassar on the basis of the number of written state-

73

ments relating to faculty rights and obligations, however, would be to overlook important differences between these institutions in (1) the manner in which written recognition has come about and (2) the role played by existing documents in the operation of each college. There is lacking at Colgate the belief that important understandings regarding faculty rights and obligations should necessarily be codified and that, conversely, important questions of faculty rights and obligations should be decided in the light of codified principles.

The difference between the type of formalization existing at Vassar and that found at Colgate is apparent in the contrast between the role of the Colgate *Faculty Handbook* and that of the Vassar *Governance*. The latter document represents codified legislation by both faculty and trustees, each provision having been formally adopted by the authority responsible for the matter with which it deals. The Colgate document is a recent product (1951) of the office of the dean of the faculty, produced on the suggestion of a few members of the faculty but not as a faculty effort. While the provisions concerning rank, tenure, and academic freedom are actually governing board legislation, most of those describing the workings of the faculty and the place of the individual within it represent one person's interpretation of accepted policy and procedure. Many of its provisions, therefore, could be questioned as not being a faithful reflection of the unwritten "constitution," whereas the validity of the corresponding provisions in the Vassar *Governance* would be unlikely to be questioned.

Another indication of the difference between the two institutions in the role played by written documents is that several Colgate faculty members indicated lack of firsthand acquaintance with the *Faculty Handbook*, and one did not know it existed. Every person encountered at Vassar had definite opinions to express about the *Governance*.

Development of the Colgate pattern

Much of the pattern of formalized rights and obligations of faculty members at Colgate is understandable in the light of

74

certain events of the two most recent administrations, that of an austere and single-minded president in the 1920's and 1930's, and that of a more liberal one since 1942. The last vestige of formal Baptist control disappeared at Colgate in 1928, when the Seminary was removed and merged with the Rochester Theological Seminary to form the Colgate-Rochester Divinity School. Baptist influences remained, however, particularly through the 1930's, in the person of President George B. Cutten, a former Baptist minister. It is said that although he did not interfere with the academic activities of individuals, his judgment of them as people was influenced by the fact that he himself was an aggressive prohibitionist and nonsmoker. That difficulties were precipitated by his action in individual cases is, therefore, understandable.

Another factor making for uneasiness in the relationship between the administration and the faculty during President Cutten's regime was his practice of performing by administrative action functions in which faculty members felt they should share. Despite profound respect on the part of the faculty for the president, who was considered essentially a just person, the faculty and individual members found themselves unable to assert what they felt to be their rightful role.

The occurrence of a number of unfortunate incidents in faculty-administration relationships during this period seems to have been largely responsible for the interest on the part of some faculty members in reducing to statutory form the principles that should govern acts of appointment and separation. The campus chapter of the American Association of University Professors, which became especially active at this time, has remained an aggressive, alert group ever since, even though faculty-administration relationships have changed profoundly.

The present tenure code, as embodied in recent legislation, was a product of planning for the postwar period. A faculty Committee on the Post-War College had been appointed to consider organizational, curricular, and other problems the university would face in this era. In 1945 the Committee found it desirable to recommend the adoption of statutory principles and procedures in certain faculty personnel matters. Accordingly, it developed

75

a complete set of recommendations, which the faculty, after revision, transmitted to the board of trustees via President Everett N. Case, who had been inaugurated in 1942. After several exchanges between the board and the faculty, also via the president, revised statements emerged that now constitute the official policies on matters of appointment, promotion, tenure, and academic freedom. President Case was a key figure in this development, since he was the sole channel of official communication between the two groups; and faculty members point out that the current provisions could never have been obtained under the previous administration, which caused so much faculty uneasiness in the 1930's. The memory of this earlier experience and the receptiveness of the new president provided favorable ground for adoption of the new measures.

Specific features of the pattern

Documents of government.—Two documents, other than the charter, are especially to be noted—the *By-Laws of the Board of Trustees* and the *Faculty Handbook*, which has already been mentioned. The *By-Laws* deal chiefly with the organization and procedures of the board itself, but two articles concern the president and faculty, respectively. The president is given sweeping powers over all educational activities and is made the executive officer for carying out "measures officially agreed upon by the Faculty concerning matters committed to the Faculty by the Board . . . ."[5] Faculty membership and the right to vote in faculty actions are also covered (see Comparative Synopsis, Items 15-*b* and 15-*c*). The faculty is assigned responsibility for prescribing courses of study and for numerous other educational matters, and, through the president and deans, for administering student discipline. No other legislation concerning the faculty appears in the *By-Laws*, except the statement that appointments shall be made by the trustees on recommendation of the president.

The *Handbook* is both a compilation of board legislation relating to the role of the faculty and an exposition of established organization, regulations, relationships, traditions, and procedures.

[5] *By-Laws of the Board of Trustees,* Art. IV.

As stated earlier, the *Handbook* is not considered a primary source of authority. It is a useful instrument for reference and general communication, particularly for new faculty members. Its authority, except for quoted board legislation and provisions lying exclusively within the province of the administration, is said to depend upon its correspondence with faculty practice.

Faculty organization and administrative procedures.—The faculty meets every month, by custom confirmed in the *Handbook*, and is subject to called meetings at the discretion of the president, according to the trustee *By-Laws*. Much of its work, however, is carried on through standing committees, the most important of which is the faculty-administration Committee on Educational Policy. This group has developed into a quasi-legislative body in that it approves the work of other committees concerned with problems of interest to the faculty as a whole. It does not advise the administration on appointment matters, although the administration has suggested that the nine elected faculty members of the Committee should be given this function. In this respect Colgate differs from the seven other institutions studied, which regularly have faculty advisory groups on matters of appointment.

The absence of an advisory committee on appointments does not indicate that the faculty is not concerned with such matters, for teaching faculty members do influence appointment decisions. Their participation is informal, however—a matter of consultation among the administrative officers concerned (department chairman, division director, dean of the faculty, and president) and those teaching faculty members in the same and related departments whose opinions seem especially relevant. Administrative officers are perhaps likely to be influenced more in their opinion of a teacher by the faculty member who is his direct superior than by anybody else; and there are alleged instances of individuals having been held back by their department chairman for personal reasons. This situation does not seem to occur very frequently, and there is no evidence of faith in solving the problem by increasing the formal participation of the faculty in general in matters of appointment and promotion. Several faculty members, some of them of junior rank, expressed a preference

77

for an effective, if occasionally arbitrary, administration over one of good intentions only—a view not encountered at Vassar.

Some faculty members had reservations regarding the manner in which committees were made up, and it was alleged at least once that diverse views were not always duly represented. In addition to the Nominating Committee itself, whose members are elected by the faculty, and the Committee on Educational Policy, which is composed partly of administrative officers ex officio and partly of elected faculty members, there appear to be only two important bodies to which faculty members are regularly elected. Although members of these and of a number of other standing committees are nominated by the Nominating Committee, the majority of committee appointments are actually made by the president with the approval of the Committee on Educational Policy. Special committees are almost invariably appointed by the president, though they may be nominated by the Nominating Committee.

One agency for the expression of faculty desires and opinions is the local chapter of the American Association of University Professors, which has remained active since the time of its partisan role in the 1930's, and whose membership includes three quarters of the faculty. Although it has standing committees on academic freedom and tenure and on salary problems, it also takes an interest in whatever problems of the college the members wish to discuss. Subjects may thus be rendered more manageable in faculty meetings because a degree of consensus has been reached outside.

The value of the AAUP chapter as a quasi-parliamentary organ is viewed with reservation by some faculty members. One reason may be that the presentation of views in the AAUP groups is based on the interests of attending members rather than on those of the faculty as a whole. Furthermore, as one professor remarked, since there is no commitment to follow-up action, views pertinent to faculty problems are sometimes aired in AAUP discussions and then dropped, instead of being introduced at faculty meetings, where they could be acted upon.

Although no effort was made to study in detail the structure and functions of academic divisions in the eight colleges, one feature of the divisional organization at Colgate deserves mention here. Whereas at several other institutions the divisions exist as curriculum-planning and operating units or as professional associations, at Colgate each division director is also a faculty personnel officer. He passes on the appointment or promotion recommendations of each department chairman in his division, consults as he sees fit, and forwards the chairman's and his own recommendations to the dean of the faculty. This process should be considered in noting the absence of formal faculty participation in appointment matters, since, of the four administrative officers involved in each decision, two (the division director and the department chairman) are also teaching faculty members and likely to have a "faculty point of view."

The departments are under the direction of the several chairmen, subject to the division directors and the dean of the faculty, and are guided by policies determined by the faculty. Several of the departments operate as informal cooperating groups, important decisions being reached by consensus rather than unilaterally. Allegedly, some departments are more rigidly controlled by senior members than others, though there is a traditional understanding that policies and appointment recommendations, for which the chairman is responsible, are made only after consultation with or polling of the other members. This understanding is reflected in one of the recommendations of the Committee on the Post-War College, one which was not formally adopted, that on matters of promotion there should be consultation with the department members of higher rank than the candidate being considered.

Issues and trends

In several of the colleges studied, including Colgate, the writer was unable to identify any major current issues relating to the role of faculty members. This does not mean that conflict is entirely absent, but that the issues about which the faculty is concerned relate, for the most part, to matters other than their role as faculty members.

79

It would appear that if confidence in the administration provides security to the faculty, the Colgate faculty enjoys a considerable measure of security. In the usually delicate area of salary, for example, nobody criticized adversely the policy of permitting overlapping between ranks, a policy attacked in two other colleges. A frequent observation was that the president was trying to have salaries raised, and the impression conveyed was that faculty members felt confident that their interests were receiving proper consideration. As in several other institutions, there was the occasional suggestion that a statute in a certain area of faculty rights was not necessary provided there was an expression of intent on the part of the administration.

The writer was interested in whether faculty members at Colgate felt the need for freer and more direct access to the trustees, since, as was mentioned in Chapter II, the other seven colleges all seemed to have better channels of communication than Colgate. During the legislative revision described on pages 75–76, the exchange of proposals and counterproposals between the board and the faculty was made entirely through the president, instead of through trustee-faculty conference groups, as it would have been in certain other institutions.

There seemed to be little tendency at Colgate to question the effectiveness of existing communication arrangements. Although there was some interest in the fact that the writer had visited institutions where faculty-trustee conference groups existed, considerable confidence was shown in the ability of the president to represent the faculty faithfully before the trustees. It was suggested by one faculty member that where there is a clear and unavoidable difference of financial interest between the two groups, rather than merely a problem of communication, direct conference may be a less constructive way of approaching the matter than the use of an "honest broker," as President Case was once described. One professor stated that he did not think it likely that a *general* trustee-faculty conference system, like that of Mount Holyoke or Vassar, would be instituted during President Case's administration, since the need for such a system would not be sufficiently felt by the faculty.

There are other indications of the stability of the currently recognized pattern of faculty rights and obligations at Colgate. At the time of the recent revisions of board legislation the faculty did not press for a larger and more formal share in the government and administration of the college. Although the Committee on the Post-War College did make many recommendations in the areas of over-all organization, faculty personnel practices, and educational policies, there was no recommendation that consideration be given to faculty representation on the board, to the establishment of a trustee-faculty conference system, or to the use of a faculty advisory body on appointments and promotions. By way of contrast, it may be noted that the two latter arrangements are in existence at most of the eight colleges, and that the former exists at two of them and is under serious discussion at one other.

Further evidence in support of this picture of equilibrium is seen in a professor's statement that today, with several key committees largely elected, the faculty is really not much better off than it was with appointed committees under the previous administration. It was also stated by two faculty members that the codification of principles relating to tenure did not represent a profound change, if indeed any, from previous conditions. Numerous other remarks confirmed the impression that the faculty was not greatly concerned about the protective value of democratic machinery and its expression in documents of government.

The reluctance to press for written embodiment of faculty personnel policies should not be mistaken for lack of interest in the policies themselves. The 1945 report of the Committee on the Post-War College proposed a number of measures affecting the rights and obligations of faculty members, which still have not been formally adopted. One recommendation was that a written review of the record of each faculty member should be presented by division directors and department heads to the dean of the faculty at least every three years, and that every faculty member should be considered for an increase in salary at least every other year. One of the proposed means of convening a faculty meeting was by petition of any ten voting members. It will be recalled that

81

provisions similar to both of these appear in the Vassar *Governance* (see pp. 62 and 64).

Despite the recent adoption of a written code concerning certain aspects of faculty members' rights and obligations, those who were interviewed at Colgate seemed to think of their rights as resting on common consent and not upon any written protection. Those whose memories included the circumstances that led to the adoption of the present code were inclined to take a longer view ahead and to emphasize its value in the event of a change in administration. Others were inclined to emphasize the satisfying quality of present administration-faculty relationships and to be relatively unconcerned about possible future developments.

SARAH LAWRENCE COLLEGE

In a number of ways Sarah Lawrence College is different from every other institution included in this study. While not all its unique features are equally relevant to this discussion, a brief enumeration of some of them is necessary in order to orient the reader.

Sarah Lawrence has no instructional ranks and, strictly speaking, no academic departments. Its curriculum is basically a student advisory system supplemented by instructional offerings, rather than the reverse, so that the teacher's instructional obligations are, to a greater extent than in the other institutions, to individual students. Sarah Lawrence is also the only institution studied in which the faculty has legal representation on the board of trustees, one trustee being elected by the board on nomination by the faculty.

Two other facts about Sarah Lawrence should be mentioned by way of introduction. The first is that this college, though the smallest of the group, has much more extensive codification of faculty rights and obligations than several of the others. The second is that at Sarah Lawrence the implementing of these provisions is more directly in the hands of the faculty than at any of the others, with the possible exception of Vassar.

82

General description

Most of the written provisions relating to rights and obligations of faculty members are contained in the *Faculty By-Laws*, a separate document from the *Sarah Lawrence College By-Laws*. The latter instrument is the principal constitutional document of the board of trustees, but it makes no reference to the topic of faculty rights and obligations except to state that the president has final authority "in the internal affairs of the College."[6] Other papers, such as a committee report adopted by the board, and a letter from the chairman of the board to the college and alumnae, are also listed in Table 1 as important documents because of the subjects with which they are concerned; the *Faculty By-Laws*, however, constitute the principal instrument whose contents deal with the topic of this study.

The *Faculty By-Laws* contain clear policies on length of appointment, manner of appointment, processes of separation, and other aspects of the teacher's relationship to the college. They also provide for the constituting of the faculty organization that administers these policies in cooperation with the administration. The only other institutions in the group that have as much prescribed machinery are Mount Holyoke and Vassar. Wesleyan has perhaps as much in writing concerning faculty organization as does Sarah Lawrence, but with the significant difference that the Wesleyan document is not a code of the faculty as a whole, and the most important committee with which it deals is not elected by the faculty. At Sarah Lawrence all standing committees are elected.

The principal difference between the treatment of faculty rights and obligations at Sarah Lawrence and at Vassar, aside from the length and detail of the documents of government, is that Sarah Lawrence does not clearly designate the respective areas of jurisdiction of trustees and of faculty. The trustees are said to approve of the internal constitution that the administration and the faculty have jointly worked out, but there is no trustee statement

[6] *Sarah Lawrence College By-Laws*, Art. IV, sec. 1.

83

as to its legality, as there is at Vassar, nor any formal stipulation of what matters must be referred to the board for approval. In fact, even faculty appointments are made by the president without referring specific actions to the board.

In several additional respects the rights and obligations of faculty members at Sarah Lawrence rest on a less formal basis than at Vassar or Mount Holyoke. Although there is much cooperation between trustees and faculty in the formulation of policies, meetings between the two groups for this purpose seem to occur regardless of whether the by-laws of either body call for them. The Committee on Academic Freedom and the Committee on Salaries and Leaves of Absence are examples of groups that advise the board without any specific authorization in the *Sarah Lawrence College By-Laws*. On the other hand, there is one specific provision for regular consultation between trustee and faculty groups that is not generally followed. This is the statement that the board's Committee on Education "shall be entrusted with formulating the educational policy of the College in consultation with the faculty."[7] Such consultation, at the time of this writing, had not taken place for at least three years, and it was the faculty, rather than the board's Committee on Education, that had formulated educational policy during that time. Finally, Sarah Lawrence, unlike several other colleges studied, has no official written recognition of continuous tenure. The right, or the privilege, of continuous tenure, however, does exist, as will be shown presently.

The over-all picture the preceding paragraphs have attempted to convey is that of an institution where faculty members are given unusual freedom to govern themselves, and in which they perform administrative functions in many areas. It is also one in which faculty authority has grown without being legally defined.

Specific features of the Sarah Lawrence pattern

The pattern of recognized rights and obligations at Sarah Lawrence is in part a legacy from Vassar, through the membership

[7] *Sarah Lawrence College By-Laws*, Art. V, sec. 2.

of President Henry Noble MacCracken of Vassar on the first Sarah Lawrence board of trustees and through a number of other Sarah Lawrence trusteeships held by Vassar people. Some features, however, are indigenous to Sarah Lawrence and derive from the particular school of thought on which, in the educational sense, the college was founded. With the Vassar heritage may be associated the systematic, written plan of faculty organization and operation. Several other colleges in the group, somewhat larger than Sarah Lawrence, consider such a degree of formality unnecessary for them. A number of the specific provisions found at Vassar to assure that the individual voice and the individual grievance will be heard are found also at Sarah Lawrence. One of these appears in none of the other six institutions—the right to a hearing by the Advisory Committee at any time. Elsewhere it was pointed out to the writer that such guarantees could be assumed without being formally stated.

The most conspicuous difference between Sarah Lawrence and the other institutions studied is the absence of instructional ranks, which dates from a proposal made by Dr. MacCracken as a board member in the early days of the college. The main purpose behind this proposal is not difficult to understand; to eliminate ranks would tend to abolish any "high seat at the table of learning," as Dr. MacCracken has described it, and, by reducing the striving for position, help to preserve the fresh eagerness characteristic of the faculty of this experimental college.

The absence of ranks, of course, places an additional responsibility on those who formulate and administer policies on appointments, since the fewer pre-established categories there are, the greater is the role of judgment. The administration of the entire area of appointments and salaries by an elected committee, together with the dean and the president, is unique among the eight colleges studied, and it seems to enjoy the support of the faculty.

The elimination of ranks and the assumption by the faculty of major responsibilities relating to appointments, salaries, and a number of other matters did not occur together. The faculty's voice in the formulation of salary policy, for example, was not great at the beginning. Other developments also came later, in-

85

cluding the unwritten but effective tenure policy. Continuous tenure was difficult to establish at Sarah Lawrence, because flexibility of course offerings and of individual students' programs, one of the basic aims of the institution, operates against the development of stable staff requirements. At least partly for this reason, continuous tenure has not been officially guaranteed. The college manages to follow, however, the tenure practices specified in the AAUP–AAC *Principles*. A four-year appointment is given to any teacher who is kept after four years,[8] and the right to a formal hearing before the Advisory Committee—a right embodied in the *Faculty By-Laws*—is assured in any case of non-reappointment, regardless of how long the faculty member has served the college. While no written provision is made for an appeal in the event of unfavorable decision by the Advisory Committee, it is understood that a further hearing would be allowed before the Standing Committee of the teaching faculty, an elected group that has no authority to act but whose stand would tend to influence administrative action.

No reference is made in either the *Sarah Lawrence College By-Laws* or the *Faculty By-Laws* to the role of the trustees in matters of involuntary termination of service. Since the president and faculty formulate the policies and make the decisions on appointments and salaries, however, the decision to terminate a faculty member's service is normally made by this group, the president's action making it official. If the college's *right* to terminate a person's service were questioned, as in the case of an unexpired contract, the board would presumably become involved. It is said, however, that this type of separation is unlikely to occur; hence, the question of what procedures would be followed is speculative.

Another area of faculty rights and obligations in which the experience of Sarah Lawrence is significant is that of academic freedom. There have been a number of controversies within the college over this subject, and external relations have been heavily affected by it recently. In spite of the occasional disputes sur-

---

[8] The first four years of service may consist of two two-year terms or of two one-year terms followed by a two-year term (see Comparative Synopsis, Item 2-*b*).

rounding academic freedom, however, a proposal to adopt detailed legislation along the lines of the AAUP–AAC *Principles* was dropped by the faculty as unnecessary. There have been official statements on the subject, and the one made in connection with an informal inquiry on the part of the local chapter of the American Legion is referred to in the Comparative Synopsis[9] as the official policy of the college. This policy excludes political affiliation as a factor in judging the fitness of a person to teach.

An elected faculty Committee on Academic Freedom is formally constituted to advise the administration and the faculty, "individually or collectively," and "to cooperate with the Board, President and the faculty in the formulation and execution of policies regarding academic freedom."[10] In setting up a committee on academic freedom, instead of passing detailed legislation about it, the Sarah Lawrence faculty seems to express the same view as in entrusting matters of reappointment and salary advancement to the Advisory Committee, with no precise formula to be applied in making decisions.

One aspect of the faculty member's obligations at Sarah Lawrence that deserves special attention is his responsibility toward students. While several other colleges in the group grant the student body a degree of self-government and prescribe certain areas of joint student-faculty jurisdiction, as does Sarah Lawrence, none of the others has as the core of the curriculum the individual student advisory program, based on the relationship of the student and her faculty adviser, or "don." Because of the importance of this aspect of the teacher's work, it is made a part of his contractual obligation to the college to act as adviser to a certain number of students. In decisions affecting the academic status of his own students, the don is entitled, according to the *Faculty By-Laws*, to vote in the Committee on Student Work, the faculty group that actually decides such questions.

The special nature of the Sarah Lawrence curriculum is recognized also in certain other faculty legislation on rights and obligations of faculty members. Every instructional program is sub-

[9] Item 9-*a*. See also Table 1.
[10] *Faculty By-Laws*, Art. II (1).

87

ject to annual review by the Committee on Curricular Problems. Furthermore, the membership of each curriculum-planning unit of the faculty is determined by the educational purposes of the activity to be planned rather than by the departmental subject area or discipline within which the activity seems most easily classified. In view of the ruling concern at Sarah Lawrence for having each course offering serve the over-all objectives of an integrated undergraduate program, it is understandable why one person maintained that there was less exercise of the teacher's individuality with respect to particular courses here than at Vassar.

Sarah Lawrence is not the only institution in the group where it was said that curriculum-planning units of the faculty were composed according to the educational activity to be planned rather than strictly according to departmental disciplines. A number of other colleges had sections of the curriculum similarly conceived, particularly Hobart, where the Coordinate Course staff in a given area is an interdepartmental group but develops an identity of its own. The complete absence of departments as administrative units at Sarah Lawrence, however, would tend to make identification with over-all instructional purposes more effective than where departmental membership also exists. At Vassar the priority of departmental claims on the teacher's work is explicit; the *Academic Statute* grants the teacher freedom in the conduct of his courses, *but* "subject to the aims of the department as a whole" (see Comparative Synopsis, Item 12-*b*).

Evaluation of the Sarah Lawrence pattern
by faculty members

The foregoing account is of an institution run primarily by its faculty, and possessing certain features of faculty control unusual even among faculty-run colleges, such as the setting of individual salaries. According to the view of one administrative officer, the lesson of the college's experience is that if a faculty is given the responsibilities it has at Sarah Lawrence, it will live up to them. Standards of teaching become the concern of faculty members, and as a result they are as desirous of seeing sound decisions made on appointments as the officers of administration.

Also, as one faculty member stated, they are not worried by the possibility that their prerogatives in administration might be taken away by action of the trustees, because the administrative work of elected faculty committees is too important. To abolish the committees, in the words of President Harold Taylor, "would cut the heart out of the college." As evidence of the aim of excellence on the part of the faculty, it was pointed out that teachers of only one year's service are sometimes elected to important policy-making committees because of the quality of their contributions to committee work.

The faculty members interviewed seemed to feel that the written guarantees of faculty rights and obligations were not lacking in anything essential, but one stated that it would be good for the morale of new members to have tenure policies confirmed in writing. "When you're new, you think about them," it was said, whereas those who have been on the faculty long enough to understand the operation of the policies take them for granted.

HAVERFORD COLLEGE

General description and principal features

The pattern of recognized faculty rights and obligations that exists today at the oldest orthodox Quaker institution[11] of higher learning in the United States is confusing if one is looking for the consistent development of a single influence. The well-known Quaker background and the small size of Haverford College combine to present, as would be expected, an informal pattern of institutional operation. In spite of this informality, however, certain principles affecting faculty rights and obligations are set forth with great care in legislation of the governing board. Furthermore, some of the subjects thus treated are among those in which Quaker principles alone would seem to suffice without the help of codification—for example, academic freedom and contracts of appointment.

Two factors largely account for this paradox. First, the reasons

[11] Founded as Haverford School in 1833; became a degree-granting institution in 1856.

89

for the enactment of the legislation are more consistent with the Quaker tradition than a mere perusal of the documents might suggest. The written formalization of understandings seems to have been a concession to the complexity of the matters involved rather than to the superiority of written guarantees over tacit understanding. Second, the leadership of the present president has been exerted to bring about formalization by statute in the areas of academic freedom and tenure. Whether this advocacy of statutory guarantees in certain areas is consistent with his characteristically Quaker approach in others is a matter of opinion, but the writer heard no criticism of inconsistency on his part.

In areas other than those in which systematic effort has been made toward codification of principles, Haverford operates rather informally, and in some respects startlingly so. The history of Haverford in this century, like that of many small colleges, has been a succession of eras of highly personalized leadership. Although all the presidents preceding Gilbert F. White were Quakers, the extent to which Quaker principles and procedures governed faculty matters varied widely. Perhaps the three most significant recent developments are (1) representation of the faculty on the board of managers, the governing board of the college; (2) establishment of Quaker consensus as the usual manner of reaching decisions in faculty meetings; and (3) formalization by statute of principles of academic freedom and tenure.

The first of these developments came about during the administration of President Felix Morley (1940–45), who preceded President White. It was difficult to determine the exact status of the practice of faculty representation on the governing board because of uncertainty among the faculty members questioned. It appears, however, that the representation has no legal standing, since it is not authorized by the charter or legislation supplemental to it. Furthermore, the two faculty members elected to this responsibility did not vote in board meetings until recently; and when they did begin to vote, the change was not marked by any formal action—they merely voted, with the approval of the legally constituted board. A still further qualification is that faculty representatives have elected alternates to attend board meetings if needed. In this respect they are not, as individuals, members of the board.

The relationship that has evolved over the past nine years between the president and the faculty representatives on the board of managers deserves special note as an illustration of the regulatory force of usage in internal operation. It has become the custom for the president to consult in advance with these faculty members on all proposals he expects to bring before the board. It is said that it would henceforth be very difficult for a president to ignore this custom.

The reason the lack of clear legality of faculty representation is not a source of controversy, according to the writer's interpretation of the explanations given, is that Quaker groups do not vote, as parliamentary bodies usually do, in order to decide a question by measurement of strength. The purpose of the vote is to help the group see how it aligns on a question, in order to facilitate progress toward consensus. Since the board and the faculty see their relationship in this way, it would be considered irrelevant to ask whether the presence of two faculty members, or their alternates, might place two legally unauthorized people in a position to influence action for which only the remaining members of the group are ultimately responsible. It was said by one faculty officer with long experience in attending board meetings that he could not remember a dissenting vote in any action taken by the board "for many years."

The second major recent development, the practice of making decisions in faculty meetings by consensus, came about in 1949 at the suggestion of President White. Since the faculty is small, attendance at the monthly meetings being about forty members, much business can easily be conducted by the group as a whole. It was explained that the change to Quaker consensus procedure was not an effort to achieve greater democracy, since fully as great a measure of democracy may exist under Robert's *Rules of Order*. It was designed rather to expedite business, and, according to the opinions heard, it has succeeded. Few, if any, matters have been put to a vote in the years since the new procedure was instituted, according to one statement.

91

The third recent development of special importance is the passing of board legislation on academic freedom and tenure, striking because of its occurrence in an institution otherwise largely devoid of formal statements of rights and obligations of faculty members. A crucial factor in this development has been the growing uneasiness, throughout the nation, about academic freedom and tenure, which caused President White to feel that in these areas policies should be more formally stated. At his instigation a board-faculty committee was designated to prepare the statement, the use of *ad hoc* joint committees being a common practice at Haverford. The provisions are, in the main, those of the AAUP–AAC *Principles,* though there was considerable adaptation of them to the Haverford context.

Other features of the Haverford pattern

Documents of government.—The charter, with supplements and amendments, makes no reference to faculty rights and obligations, except to charge the board of managers with responsibility for the government of the institution, including the appointment of teachers and other officers. The brief *By-Laws of the Corporation* likewise contain little of relevance to this study. Unlike the by-laws of several of the other governing boards, they contain no reference to the status or functions of the faculty or its members. The faculty itself, moreover, does not in general codify its proceedings. Hence, the written provisions that are reported in this study are taken from various documents such as the administrative bulletin, *Information for Members of the Faculty,* which includes the managers' "Statement on Academic Freedom and Tenure."

It may be useful to compare the written provisions found at Haverford with those found at Colgate, though the Haverford statements are not as extensive. Both institutions have considerable formal legislation on academic freedom and tenure and succinct statements on salary scale, dismissal, and one or two other matters, while a number of areas, such as faculty participation in academic government, are left mainly to custom.

The bulk of codified legislation concerning faculty rights and obligations that has been passed by the board of managers is contained in the board's 1950 "Statement on Academic Freedom and Tenure," which has already been mentioned. This statement forms part of the bulletin, *Information for Members of the Faculty,* which is a compilation of board, administration, and faculty regulations and of routine information. The bulletin does not contain all existing written rules, and two references are made in it to other documents containing important policy statements by the administration.

One provision that appears in the bulletin mentioned above is noteworthy because it goes beyond the concept of academic freedom as usually expressed. It is a policy statement by the faculty, which encourages members of the faculty and the administration to take an active part as citizens "in public movements controversial or otherwise."[12] Compared with statements in the other colleges on the obligations relating to academic freedom, this statement of the Haverford faculty is noteworthy for the implication that it is necessary to promote the exercise of the teacher's freedom as a citizen, and not merely to protect this freedom when it is exercised.[13] This is the most positive reference encountered in the study to the kind of citizen the teacher should be.

Faculty organization and administrative procedures.—The administrative procedures affecting the appointment status of individual faculty members are largely unwritten, and in this respect they are unlike those of Mount Holyoke, Sarah Lawrence, Vassar, or Wesleyan. They are unlike the procedures employed at Colgate in that committees are used in appointment and promotion decisions, teaching faculty members being regularly included in such bodies. The Haverford system is in some respects

[12] "There is a need at all times, but particularly in times of crisis, for intelligent persons to make their considered opinions known both to their legislative representatives and to the voting public. Members of the Faculty and Administration should, therefore, be commended for taking an active part as citizens, either singly or in groups, in public movements controversial or otherwise."—Faculty minutes for March 20, 1941, as quoted in *Information for Members of the Faculty.*

[13] The writer is not unmindful of the distinction between academic freedom in the strict professional sense and the freedom the academic person shares with all other citizens. This stand of the Haverford faculty is cited here as relating to academic freedom in the *broad* sense, which includes the scholar's rights and obligations both as a citizen and as a member of his profession and his institution.

93

similar to the advisory-council system at Hobart, except that at Haverford the procedure is more variable. Recommendations on reappointments and promotions are determined by the Administrative Committee, consisting of the president, the vice-president, the dean, and ordinarily the two faculty representatives on the governing board. An *ad hoc* committee, however, may be used to advise this group if a decision is difficult to reach. Decisions in practice are by consensus, as in other areas of faculty administration at Haverford, although they are the final responsibility of the president. Because of the small size of the faculty and the ease of casual communication, consultation is apparently so readily accomplished that some of the formal guarantees made at other colleges to assure it are not considered necessary here.

Other procedures need not be described in detail, the main characteristics being (1) informality and (2) decisions by consensus. Faculty and administration work closely together, defined power counting for little. There are no important standing representative committees, as there are at Mount Holyoke, Vassar, Sarah Lawrence, and Wesleyan. In this respect, as may be seen in the portions of the Comparative Synopsis dealing with Swarthmore, the two Quaker institutions are alike. The Academic Council at Haverford, consisting of the three chief administrative officers and three elected faculty members, appears in principle to resemble the pivotal Advisory Council at Hobart, or some of the key advisory groups in other institutions. Actually, however, the functions of the Academic Council are relatively minor. It advises the president on appointments to faculty committees and may grant waivers on such academic regulations as the faculty itself does not administer by direct action. The need for a top-level advisory group in many administrative areas is apparently obviated by the ability of the faculty and the president to act together as a working group.

Evaluation of the Haverford pattern by faculty members

The comments made by faculty members on the manner in which their rights and obligations are recognized and imple-

94

mented were, on the whole, very favorable. One professor observed that the board's principal published legislation, the "Statement on Academic Freedom and Tenure," would help a new president to know what he had inherited. Favorable comments were also made concerning other policy statements, such as that on faculty housing, a matter that had caused controversy in earlier years.

The value of written commitments for clarity and for dissemination of information about basic policies was occasionally mentioned. This fact is especially worthy of note in a small institution, and in one where procedures are generally very informal. The strictly protective value of the written promise did not seem a major concern, and the main evidence that protection was an important factor was the statement by the president that a certain restlessness and insecurity regarding tenure had been part of the reason for the legislation of policies in that area.

There are, of course, still sources of dissatisfaction and insecurity. The pre-tenure period is bound to be an insecure one, and there was some feeling that qualifications for promotion were surrounded with unnecessary and disturbing vagueness. A number of people, however, not all of whom had tenure, felt that more explicit official commitments, and consequent loss of flexibility in appointment policies, would operate to the disadvantage of the college.

The attitude of the faculty toward increasing formalization of its rights may be summarized in the statements of two of its members. One said that as long as President White held office, it would be a definite *disadvantage* to have certain rights more formally stated, since, where there is a rule, administrative action can be no more liberal than the rule permits, whereas President White's decisions could be counted on to be as liberal as the merits of the situation allowed. For this particular institution, the other faculty member said, the advantages of protection against possible future infringement, through the addition of further written guarantees, would not be worth the decrease in flexibility that would result, nor the risk of losing the present atmosphere of trust among faculty, administration, and board.

95

Trends at Haverford

It is evident from the preceding account that there is a strong belief on the part of the Haverford faculty in sound personal relationships and in the effectiveness of principles and procedures that evolve under the influence of such relationships. Given this belief, the faculty is not inclined to seek protection of its interests in governing documents. There have been movements toward such formalization, however, initiated under the impact of outside forces or of a specific internal situation. The recent revision of *Information for Members of the Faculty*, by its inclusion of policies on such matters as sabbatical leave, attests to the need for written commitments in certain areas hitherto left to tacit understanding. It would appear that the general reluctance to have matters prescribed in official documents is a relative one and that, for sufficient reason, specific additions to the existing body of written regulations may be expected from time to time.

There was apparently more confidence at Haverford than at some of the other colleges in the effectiveness of existing safeguards of academic freedom against invasion by outside investigating committees. The writer was told that there had been no discussion as yet of what the college's policy was to be if a faculty member refused to testify before congressional groups, though one member had already been called to testify. It was said that the board of managers includes such influential people that it would be difficult for the college to be successfully attacked by the publicizing of unfounded charges.

CHAPTER IV

IMPLICATIONS
FOR COLLEGE GOVERNMENT
AND ADMINISTRATION

Diversity of Patterns Found

The purpose of this chapter is to identify the principal findings of the study and to relate them to problems of college government and administration. There is naturally very limited potential for generalization in material gathered from only eight institutions; hence, the interpretations presented here are offered cautiously.

One of the aims of the study was to determine the extent to which the rights and obligations of faculty members in the eight colleges were formalized in documents and in prescribed policies and procedures. Firmly established, though unwritten, regulations on the one hand, and statutory enactments of the trustees on the other, were taken to represent differing degrees of formality, and the basis of each recognized right or obligation was examined to determine both its stated and its actual status in the life of the institution.

There is no single criterion for determining whether a right or obligation is officially recognized or not. If recognition is based on an act of the trustees, of course, or of a person or group authorized by the trustees to act with respect to the policy area in question, such a right or obligation must be considered official. Often, however, the line of delegated authority from the trustees to the administration and faculty is not explicitly established but has developed through usage, just as certain rights and obligations of individuals have developed through usage.[1] Hence, a given principle or practice established by the administration or faculty or a part thereof may be formally recognized and thoroughly effective without having any statutory status. Naturally the force of such a principle is often difficult to establish and is occasionally a subject of disagreement within a college.

There is little uniformity among the colleges studied as to titles or contents of documents of government bearing upon faculty rights and obligations. Although several of the charters refer briefly to matters affecting rights of faculty members, and although all eight governing boards have by-laws of their own, most of the subjects with which this study is concerned are treated more extensively in other documents.[2] Board legislation relating to faculty rights and obligations may either be found in systematically codified statements or may find its way into more casual instruments, such as bulletins of information. Except for such matters as pensions and other employee benefits, there is no single right or obligation recognized in an officially published instrument in all eight institutions.

The contents of the documents vary not only in scope but also in emphasis. Among those institutions that do have a relatively large amount of written prescription of faculty rights and obligations, Colgate has more provisions concerning academic

[1] The faculties of Mount Holyoke and Vassar have a clearly statutory delegation of authority, with the respective areas of board and faculty jurisdiction set forth in detail. In the other six colleges these divisions are less clearly defined, if, indeed, they are defined at all.

[2] Hobart is an exception to this statement, most of the written rights and obligations found there being stated in the *By-Laws of the Colleges of the Seneca*. There is also much important legislation concerning faculty rights and obligations in the *By-Laws of the Trustees of Mount Holyoke College*.

98

freedom and tenure than any other area. Sarah Lawrence has more provisions concerning the internal organization of the faculty, and Vassar has extensive written provisions in all areas, including several unique guarantees to the individual against neglect or injustice.

MANNER IN WHICH OFFICIAL RECOGNITION HAS DEVELOPED

A variety of processes has contributed to the development of the several patterns of officially recognized rights and obligations that were found. Provisions have either been formally legislated or (in a few cases) set to writing as interpretations of established practice. Sometimes they have been adopted as entire codes; sometimes they have grown by repeated revision. Many provisions are the product of joint trustee-faculty action rather than of action by one group or the other.[3] Boards and faculties, of course, have their respective areas of cognizance, whether officially defined or not, and where there is no overlapping between them, there is presumably no need for consultation. However, some kind of trustee-faculty cooperation in preparing board legislation affecting the faculty seems to be much more common, among the colleges studied, than unilateral action by the board.

Certain factors were found to be associated with the tendency toward written formalization, either by their presence in institutions that had highly formal patterns or by their mention, in particular situations, as factors in the development of such written provisions as there were. In several colleges this development has been stimulated by the favorable attitude of the president; and it seems to have been prevented or postponed in certain other colleges by the opposition of the president. Previous experience of the faculty with a tyrannical administration has sometimes motivated a move toward a more formal statement of teachers' rights and obligations. Conditions outside the institution have

---

[3] E.g., "Statement on Academic Freedom and Tenure," at Haverford; the *By-Laws of the Colleges of the Seneca* (sections dealing with faculty appointment matters); and the *Governance of Vassar College*.

stimulated such a movement in several colleges, especially in the areas of academic freedom and tenure. The AAUP–AAC *Principles* affected thinking in these areas considerably, as evidenced by their adoption in several of the colleges studied.[4] Also, congressional investigations of allegedly subversive influences in institutions of higher education may be expected to produce new interpretations of existing principles of teachers' rights and obligations, and perhaps even the formulation of principles hitherto unstated.

The fact that a college is a women's college, or has a predominantly female faculty, may be still another factor tending toward greater written formalization of rights and obligations. The two colleges having the most formal patterns in this respect are women's colleges. Furthermore, the remaining women's college in the group, although the smallest in enrollment, has more written provisions for faculty participation in the direction of the institution than any of the four men's colleges or the one coeducational.

A number of factors, besides the opposition of the president, seem to be associated with lack of written formalization. Faculties enjoying a heritage of satisfactory informal relationships with their trustees seem to feel that informal patterns are best for them. The fact of religious connection is related inversely to extent of formalization of faculty rights and obligations, though no causal relationship suggests itself. The three women's colleges, already mentioned as the most formal in one important sense, have always been independent of sectarian control; the three least formal are also the three that have and always have had a sectarian connection; and the two occupying an intermediate position in this respect are institutions that have had religious connections in the past but are now entirely secular. To generalize upon this finding, in view of the many other respects in which

---

[4] The AAUP–AAC *Principles*, as a whole or in part, verbatim or approximately, are incorporated in official statements of faculty personnel policy at Colgate, Haverford, and Mount Holyoke. Less explicitly, they enter into the conscious policy at Hobart, Sarah Lawrence, Swarthmore, and Wesleyan. The Vassar policy statement antedates the AAUP–AAC *Principles*.

100

these eight institutions differ from one another, would require the examination of facts beyond those gathered.

Another factor that seems to have retarded written recognition of rights and obligations in one or more colleges is the existence of more immediate problems that prevent this matter from getting much attention. It is also possible that in certain colleges there is still a sufficient measure of control by a limited group to block changes that would be to the group's disadvantage. Whenever this situation exists, it is, of course, evidence of the value of written understandings, since a written commitment would increase the difficulty of concealing authoritarian intent.

WRITTEN COMMITMENTS
VS. LESS FORMAL UNDERSTANDINGS

In addition to the interest in how official recognition of rights and obligations has come about, an important aim of the study was to examine the alleged merits of the various patterns encountered. It was desired to determine to what extent the experience of these eight colleges supports the contention that rights and obligations of faculty members should be formalized in written understandings. In the following pages the arguments that bear upon this question will be presented and appraised. It is pertinent at this point to call attention to the fact that the study is concerned with the entire range of rights and obligations of faculty members as they are understood in any college, and not only with the particular aspects a person interviewed may have had in mind while discussing the subject with the writer. Through-out the account that follows, therefore, frequent discrimination will be made between arguments affecting rights and obligations of the faculty member as an individual and those affecting the rights and obligations of the faculty as an organization.

One general observation to be made is that teachers and ad-ministrative officers tend to endorse the extent of written formali-zation characteristic of their own institution, those who live under highly formal patterns tending in general to favor more extensive

101

written formalization than those whose institutions have fewer written guarantees. An exception to this tendency, however, is the widespread evidence of insecurity associated with the lack of a published salary scale, regardless of prevailing opinion on other aspects of the existing pattern.

Arguments in favor of written guarantees

Written guarantees as protection.—Perhaps the first benefit one might see in the written commitment of the college regarding a faculty member's rights and obligations would be his legal protection against arbitrary dismissal. The writer is inclined, however, to view this value as of small importance in the group of institutions studied. Not only are dismissals and forced resignations very rare, as previously shown, but trustee legislation is revocable and, hence, can provide little legal assurance that in the long run tenure policies will remain unchanged. Colgate does have a provision stating that future changes in tenure rules may not operate to deprive any appointee of tenure earned under the present rules, but this is the only guarantee found in the eight colleges against loss of rights through retroactive legislation. Repeatedly the assertion was made, throughout the colleges having relatively few written guarantees, that a clear statement of intent by the administration or trustees would constitute assurance as convincing as a statute.

To rule out the legal aspect of protection as relatively insignificant, however, does not make the protective value of written commitments unimportant, and much support was found, especially in the colleges having a large number of such provisions, for the protective value of the written word. Where the rights of the faculty as a body are concerned, an action that directly violated a clear commitment by the trustees or administration could easily be made self-defeating by the united opposition it would arouse. Trustees and faculties have to get along with each other, and any formalization of understanding that makes the transgressing of rights more difficult to conceal adds to the stability of those rights. As far as the individual faculty member is concerned, the *clarity* of a right, resulting from its being set to

102

writing, is also a protective factor, regardless of whether the right in question is legally enforceable. This advantage of the written word was admitted to be a relative one. It was not contended, for example, that a junior member of a traditionally autocratic department could expect to be treated entirely in accordance with the spirit of a liberal faculty constitution, in view of the difficulty of legislating the behavior of departments.

The foregoing considerations apply chiefly to the protection of the faculty and its members. It is also possible, however, for statutory commitments by the trustees to be a protection to the administration and even to the trustees themselves, when it is necessary to meet public or other pressure running contrary to the conscientious judgment of the institution. If a professor, for example, were propounding unpopular views and causing an irresponsible minority in the community to demand his dismissal, a legal commitment regarding the professor's rights and obligations might be a more effective defense of the college's action than an effort to present the merits of the case to an excited public.

Written guarantees as an aid to communication.—The value of improved communication is distinguishable from that of protection as described above in that rights may be lost through uncertainty and confusion as well as through deliberate disregard. Perhaps the most obvious advantage of reducing well-understood rules and policies to writing is the help this gives to new faculty members. Indeed, a member of one of the less formally organized faculties stated to the writer that, as a new instructor, he had found the absence of information about his place in the institution distinctly unpleasant, as had his colleagues.

Written instruments dealing with rights and obligations were felt to be useful also in preserving the spirit of understandings throughout periods of change, particularly change in administration. It is obviously desirable for a new president to know the situation he has inherited.

Communication is said to be an important advantage of written commitments in still another sense—the mutual education occurring when groups endeavor cooperatively to clarify their relationships. Any activity which brings groups face to face helps

103

them to understand each other's point of view, so that, as one faculty member stated, they tend less to treat each other as stereotypes.

Written guarantees as an aid to orderliness and consistency.— In addition to the advantages of protection and communication, there was occasionally mentioned the value of orderliness and consistency. The former president of one college stated that he had encouraged the written embodiment of policies and commitments because he did not trust his own memory. Faculties as well as administrations may act inconsistently if they are not made aware of the relation of previous actions to the issues at hand. The complaint was even voiced, in one institution, that the absence of written rules available to all tended to place the people who did know the rules in a very powerful position. A member of an important faculty committee in one college said, also, that in cases of close decisions affecting the careers of individuals, as in matters of promotion or fellowship awards, it was useful to have written statements of policy to minimize the subjective factors involved.

Arguments opposing written guarantees

*Written guarantees as superfluous.—*The various arguments offered in opposition to the formalization of rights and obligations in written commitments may be divided into (1) those finding such written forms unnecessary and (2) those considering them positively harmful. Arguments of the first group are generally based on the supposed strength of tradition and usage. It was pointed out in one institution, for example, that the document setting forth faculty policies and practices was merely a *post factum* interpretation by one person, and that its validity depended on its correspondence with actual practice.

It was pointed out in several colleges that individuals as well as the faculty as a whole were well protected by firmly established and understood principles regarding promotion, determination of educational policies, and other matters of concern to faculty members. While the unwritten academic constitution of tradition and usage was certainly in evidence at many points in the adminis-

104

tration of these eight colleges, it was by no means apparent to the writer that it covered effectively all areas of rights and obligations. There were enough criticisms, in the colleges lacking most of the written guarantees, to suggest strongly that even if the rights of all were scrupulously observed, the lack of appreciation of that fact in certain quarters of the faculty testified at least to absence of proper communication. Under these circumstances it hardly seems defensible to dismiss written formalization as superfluous.

The writer concurs with many of the comments made by people he interviewed, to the effect that the strength of custom and tradition was sufficient to guarantee the effectiveness of certain important rights and obligations. This concurrence, however, he limits to specific situations to which the remarks were addressed. He does not feel that the evidence gathered supports any *general* conclusion that tradition may be exclusively relied on. The force of an unwritten constitution, or of any norm existing only in the minds of people, is dependent upon its opportunity to become "internalized," or assimilated, by those who are to implement it. No presumption as to its effectiveness should be made, therefore, without consideration of the rate of turnover in the board, the administration, and the faculty, and of the extent of contact the members of each group have with each of the areas in which unwritten principles are supposed to operate. In short, if there is an invisible force of considerable importance, just who embodies it, and how, and wherein lies its stability?

As to the argument, frequently heard, that all these matters are well understood anyway, suffice it to say that in more than one of the colleges studied one has merely to turn to the junior members of the faculty to be told that this is often not so. Matters such as the relative weight of various criteria in determining fitness for promotion, factors affecting individual salaries, and the role of junior ranks in determining educational policies are among the important questions about which one receives sharply conflicting reports within the same institution. Clearly, the argument that written commitments in such areas are superfluous is not to be accepted without qualifications.

105

Written guarantees as harmful.—In certain areas written guarantees, if they exist, are necessarily accompanied by formally prescribed committees and procedures and, in general, by what was occasionally described as "machinery." This condition is associated in the minds of many with indirection and inefficiency. Efficiency in college government and administration is admittedly a desirable objective, but it should hardly be the ruling consideration in determining how the rights and obligations of people are to be safeguarded. Expediency may not be on the side of ultimate effectiveness.

Written formalization of the role of the faculty in administration may be opposed by faculty members themselves on the ground that, since they have ample opportunity for such participation on an informal basis, any involvement in formal machinery is an unnecessary nuisance. This view is exemplified in the quip of a department chairman at a large university, who once told the writer that his colleagues wanted "as few rights and responsibilities as possible," as long as the administration's conduct of the institution did not offend them personally. The tradition still exists, apparently, that the scholar is the ruler of an independent duchy within the academic empire.

A question of educational philosophy, referred to in Chapter I, is involved here. The writer's premise is that members of the faculty, particularly teaching members, are partners with the administration and the trustees in a common venture, and as such are concerned with matters broader than their devotion to a special field, or even to the cause of scholarship in general.[5] If this premise is accepted, participation in the direction of the institution—responsible and sustained, not casual participation—is a responsibility, not merely a right. Furthermore, this kind of participation cannot be relied upon to develop out of tradition and

[5] Ordway Tead's remarks are pertinent here: "I confess that I am still shocked to see how relatively little the ordinary faculty member seems to be concerned about *college education as a whole.* . . . not the least of the values of having continuous and rotating faculty committees on long-range curricular planning is the incentive they supply to committee members to take an inclusive and not a departmental view of what the steps ahead in higher education should be."— *Trustees, Teachers, Students: Their Role in Higher Education,* 1951, p. 109.

usage, for, as was pointed out in Chapter I, tradition and usage are too often opposed to it.

A second alleged disadvantage of written provisions concerning faculty rights and obligations is their inflexibility. This disadvantage is really a relative one, and a number of the people who mentioned it also admitted that certain types of guarantees were of value. Others, however, maintained that the criticism of inflexibility applied even to such vital matters as academic freedom, tenure, and salary. A comment typical of this view, which was not confined to either senior or junior ranks, was, "Once you have a rule, you're stuck with it, no matter what the circumstances of any case that may arise under it."

The argument that flexibility of procedure must be preserved is undoubtedly valid for certain matters, but it should not be applied sweepingly to any of the areas with which this study is concerned. Wherever this reasoning is advanced with respect to conditions of appointment, promotion, and salary, for example, it should be carefully considered whether the college is reserving to itself more freedom than sound administration should require, and whether it is thereby forcing the faculty member to assume a risk that should not be entirely his—for example, the possibility that a last-minute drop in enrollment may remove the need for his services. Furthermore, having a policy to live up to need not tie the administration's hands completely. A statement of policy may be made so flexible, through qualifying phrases such as "in general," "insofar as possible," and the like, as to constitute merely a statement of good faith.

A third objection to written guarantees in general is the alleged proliferating tendency of any body of recorded rules. Once the principle of written recognition of rights and obligations is accepted, there is naturally a tendency to regard the absence of a particular provision as significant. One administrative officer described an incident that emphasized this point. When the practice was established of sending formal notification of the president's recommendation of reappointment, there was uneasiness on the part of one faculty member because the notification made no mention of his expected salary raise. It had to be explained to him that, while the president's recommendation was tantamount to a reappointment, it remained for later board action on the budget to determine its financial terms. The administrative officer pointed out to the writer that, when absence of notification to the contrary was taken as assurance of reappointment, this type of difficulty did not arise. It was the existence of one written guarantee that prompted the individual to look for others.

The possibility that written formalization may lead to further written formalization is supported to some extent by other statements relating to the manner in which written guarantees have developed. As successive editions of a document are worked out, specific items are added to meet new contingencies. Faith in the effectiveness of the printed word grows; and since some parts of the document have become more specific than others, the inference is that the "vague" sections should be made more explicit. Since there is no corresponding factor tending toward simplification, dependence on the coverage of details by the document tends to increase indefinitely, resulting in an inflexible instrument.

It seems to the writer that this disadvantage could be avoided if (1) the function of the written framework of guarantees were clearly understood and (2) proposed amendments were examined to determine whether they were sufficiently basic to deserve to be included, or whether their purpose could properly be served by embodiment in some subordinate instrument of particulars, such as an information bulletin.

A fourth criticism, one offered particularly by administrators, was that codification of such matters as faculty rights and obligations might damage relationships among board, administration, and faculty. The proposal to codify an existing policy on academic freedom, for example, might be taken as an admission that the government of the institution was not trusted to maintain such a policy otherwise. The values of long-range protection, to be gained by a more explicit expression of rights and obligations, would have to be balanced against the strained relationships that might be brought about by the suggestion that such protection was desirable. One of the presidents offered the view, moreover, that the adoption of official standards in such matters tends "to set a ceiling as well as a floor" to the efforts of all parties to live up to their responsibilities.

One situation in which strained relationships were aggravated, apparently, by the existence of a highly formal system resulted from the disfranchising of certain professional appointments at Vassar through an amendment to the *Academic Statute*. Present holders of the appointments in question were not affected by the change, since it included a clause specifically exempting them from the loss of voting privileges due to the amendment. Nevertheless, the fact that their offices had been formally relegated to a nonvoting class had a status meaning for these appointees, which need not have been so blunt but for the fact of its embodiment in the *Academic Statute*.

Further qualifications

The views mentioned in the two preceding sections were clearly favorable or unfavorable to the written formalization of personal and group relationships within the institution. A number of additional opinions seem important, although they neither favor nor oppose written formalization per se but rather represent qualifications of the various principal arguments, according to the conditions faced by the college in question. A view frequently encountered, perhaps especially among members of departments of history and government, was that legislated provisions concerning such matters as faculty rights and obligations should be confined to the main principles involved, and that no effort should be made to codify exact administrative procedures. Principles plus interpretations, it was said, constitute a pattern just as sound and considerably more flexible than the kind of "catch-all" document that cumulative effort at precision tends to produce.

It was expected that the size of an institution would be found to play an important part in determining the need for written formalization, and several opinions confirmed this view. Furthermore, the number of actual written provisions encountered bears a certain relation to enrollment, the largest institutions having the most extensive official documents. The relationship is not consistent throughout the group, however, as has been pointed out

109

in Chapter III; hence the factor of size should not be over-emphasized.

The remarks of some faculty and administrative officers seemed to suggest that although they favored much of the written constitutional structure under which they lived, they did not consider this aspect of the pattern to be of primary value. Even at Vassar, where the writer found more zeal for written guarantees than anywhere else, it was said, "The *Governance* merely embodies the spirit of things that *work*." Another comment from Vassar, in the same vein, was that a document embodying things people believe in can become the focus of a cohesive loyalty, as the United States Constitution is in our national life. A number of findings throughout this study have emphasized the importance of relating the formal structure to the organic whole of the life of the institution.

It must be acknowledged that there are some areas of faculty rights and obligations in which rules are unenforceable. It is not necessary, however, that the written expression be a closely regulatory instrument. In departmental affairs, for example, one of the areas apparently least accessible to legislation, it would seem that a strong written expression of general principles, by reminding people of what is expected of them and by facilitating the formation of group pressure upon individuals inclined to violate such principles, might have a salutary long-range effect. It might assist the administration and faculty, moreover, in their general approach to the filling of department chairmanships.[6]

There are other areas in which principles may, in the writer's opinion, be usefully expressed without having their implications prescribed in detail. The question of what qualifications and conditions are requisite for promotion, for example, cannot be answered in very specific terms. Some institutions do try, however,

---

[6] Some policies affecting departmental operation, of course, are readily enforceable, such as filling the chairmanship by rotation or election. In departments so small as to afford little or no opportunity for choice among eligible senior members, however, such practices are meaningless. The question may be raised whether academic departments in the usual sense constitute the most effective administrative units, a question largely outside the scope of this study. The apparent success of Sarah Lawrence, however, in dispensing with departments as administrative units invites serious consideration of this solution to problems inherent in the departmental type of faculty organization.

to state their promotion policies in writing, and it seems that the gesture is useful in communicating to the faculty the spirit in which the matter of promotions is approached.

APPARENT TRENDS
IN THE WRITTEN FORMALIZATION
OF RIGHTS AND OBLIGATIONS

To the extent that generalizations based on a study of eight institutions are significant for the study of colleges and universities in general, it may be stated that there appears to be a tendency to formalize in writing faculty rights and obligations regarding which there is pressure affecting the institution from outside. Of the six colleges having no comprehensive statutes on academic freedom and tenure before 1947, two have since adopted rather extensive codes on these subjects. At least one other institution has prepared an official statement of its position concerning the behavior of faculty members in the event of their involvement in a public investigation, such as a congressional inquiry into subversive activities. One institution, which has at the moment no such document prepared and no legislation on academic freedom, is considering in trustee-faculty conferences the stand it will take if the investigations begin to involve its faculty members.

Another trend noticeable among these eight colleges, although qualified by distinct exceptions, is a growth in the concept of "partnership" of faculty, administration, and trustees, as recognized in concrete procedures. Trustee-faculty conferences have increased in recent years in several colleges, and no cases of the reverse tendency were found, even though conference procedures are not always officially prescribed and prescribed procedures are not always observed. In most of the institutions studied the conference system, whether a statutory requirement or not, was said to be an outstanding, if not *the* outstanding, factor in sound relationships, and it was in some colleges the major source of whatever feeling of security faculty members had. The practice of faculty representation on the board was instituted in recent years

111

in two colleges, by trustee statute at Sarah Lawrence and by informal practice at Haverford. Such representation has also been under consideration at Mount Holyoke.

The partnership of faculty and administration is recognized in practice and legislation by a number of colleges. In other colleges there are at least some suggestions of increasing faculty participation in areas previously reserved for the administration and the board, though the new practice is not formalized in any permanent documents of government and is experimental in two cases.[7]

In the writer's opinion, the trends just discussed do not indicate a growing recognition that rights and obligations of faculty members ought, in general, to be more highly formalized than they are. In spite of major developments in this direction, traceable to specific causes, there seems to be no tendency toward change in the divergent points of view that characterize the various faculties.

One general consideration minimizing the significance of the specific changes discussed is the fact that some of them have taken place during or following a notable growth in the size of the institution. It seems reasonable to suppose, as a number of faculty members stated, that the size of a college is a factor in determining the extent to which its pattern of relationships, including faculty rights and obligations, should be formalized. Mount Holyoke and Vassar, the two colleges that have had rather formal patterns for the longest period of time, are the two that, at least until World War II, always had the largest enrollments in the group. Colgate, the school now second in enrollment among the eight, is the one that had the greatest *increase* in written prescriptions after World War II.

Since all eight institutions have grown in size over several decades, some of them particularly during and immediately following the war, recent efforts toward written formalization may represent in part a subconscious recognition that less formal pat-

---

[7] I.e., the faculty committee to study the cost of the educational program at Swarthmore, and the administration-faculty discussions of the role of the faculty in the building-fund drive at Haverford. The third example referred to is the established Consultative Finance Committee at Wesleyan.

terns have been outgrown. It is worth noting that at one college, where criticism of administration-faculty communication and of faculty personnel policies was frequent, several members referred nostalgically to an earlier administration, during which, with a smaller organization, the informal pattern that was an object of their present complaints had operated with great success. When the possible effect of growth in size is discounted, then, the results of the study do not indicate increasing interest in prescriptive documents in general, but rather in written clarification of such matters as academic freedom, in which, as has been observed, colleges have been under special pressures due to external conditions.

CONCLUSIONS

In any study based partly on concrete documentary material and partly on subjective data analyzed and interpreted by one person, the ideas that emerge naturally have a wide range of conclusiveness. Accordingly, the points that appear to follow clearly from evidence presented are stated first, and the writer's more personal and tentative conclusions follow.

It is to be emphasized that this study was not based on any assumptions as to what the rights and obligations of faculty members should be. It was considered sufficient (1) to accept the fact that the college faculty member has a particular role to play in our society and (2) to postulate as the rights and obligations of that role those that were recognized in the provisions and practices of the institutions being studied. There has been, furthermore, no attempt to establish a standard, either prefatory to the inquiry or issuing from it, as to which matters of rights and obligations should be officially prescribed, and in how much detail. To the extent that the study has suggested answers to this question, the sources have been largely the interpretations and opinions of various people concerning the experience of their institution. The satisfaction of the faculty, as expressed in such opinions, would naturally be one of the criteria of an effective system, since a certain security and feeling of belongingness are

113

presumed to be vital to productive work. Satisfaction of the faculty, however, cannot be the sole measure, for the faculty member's need for security and status may overrule his concern for the effectiveness of the work of the institution. It seems, in fact, that no single answer can be given to the question of what matters should be prescribed and codified.

Written commitments as an ally of sound relationships

In the light of the foregoing remarks, and on the basis of the material recorded in Chapters II and III, it may be said that there is a distinct place for official documents setting forth the rights and obligations of faculty members. There are situations where the values of such instruments have long been recognized and are deeply felt, among members of both faculty and administration. First, although the legal standing of a right may be of little importance to the faculty member, the feeling is often strong that the recorded commitment of the institution to certain principles and procedures constitutes an important protection against a lapse of observance, whether from willful abrogation or from neglect.

Second, the value of formal documents in promoting understanding of the various rights and obligations of the individual is clearly established by the testimony of faculty members in a number of institutions. While there was criticism of the extreme detail with which certain matters were specified, the value of written commitments as an aid to communication was convincingly apparent in some situations.

Third, the contribution of written policy commitments to orderliness and consistency appears unquestionable, despite the fact that some matters seem not to lend themselves to exact prescription. These three generalizations apply to the teacher's rights and obligations in his relationships with his governing board, his administrative officers, and the various organs of faculty self-government. The statement that these positive values exist does not imply that each one is necessarily to be realized in all areas of faculty rights or in all institutions. It means that

114

the values of written formalization have been strongly indicated in a variety of contexts.

Extent and pattern of formalization
as an individual matter for each college

It is also apparent that the values to which written formalization of rights and obligations contributes often do not lie in the existence or contents of documents themselves. Even in the most formal institutional situations it was repeatedly said that the real basis of effectiveness was not in the written instruments but in the common recognition of principles and relationships that the instruments helped to express. Not only are governing documents not a substitute for sound relationships; reliance on them may also involve certain risks and disadvantages. The resulting inflexibility and proliferation of rules, the temptation to solve by codified compromise issues that have not really been resolved, and the generating of the misconception that if written guarantees are valid, unwritten ones cannot be—these and other possible disadvantages of a pattern of written guarantees require continued vigilance of the institution that would make best use of it.

It is to be asked, then, on what basis the advantages of a written expression of faculty rights and obligations outweigh the advantages of an implicit one, in view of the qualifications just mentioned. The experiences reported in this study suggest that each college must determine for itself to what extent and in what areas it may gain the benefits realized by certain of these eight institutions. One college may find that, for reasons peculiar to its own situation, policies governing promotion should be stated in a trustee statute, while another may find such provisions unnecessary but feel the need for trustee prescription regarding the formulation of educational policy. No "correct" amount of codification exists for any subject or for any institution. The task of a particular college is to act in each area as seems appropriate to its character and needs and to be aware of the limitations and the problems typical of the position it assumes, whether this position is a relatively formal or a relatively informal one.

115

THE WRITER'S POSITION

The writer himself takes the position that in all the matters of rights and obligations considered in this study, and particularly in certain areas to be emphasized presently, the positive values of written formalization invite serious consideration. While it is possible for a college to do without such measures and still maintain sound relationships, such relationships should never be *presumed* to exist. The decision to rely on the strength of tradition or other relatively intangible forces should be a positive, not a negative, decision, and the burden of proof is upon whoever ventures the sweeping assertion that none of the values claimed for formal documents is applicable to his institution. Regardless of the numerous reservations, recorded throughout this report, suggesting that rights and obligations are best left to unwritten understandings, the fact is that the faculty members interviewed who were actually living under written codes did not as a group share this view. Although they did, in each institution, acknowledge certain disadvantages of their system in practice, their criticism did not extend to the system as a whole, either in principle or in practice.

A number of the conspicuously cited disadvantages of such formal situations, moreover, did not seem to the writer to be inherent in the fact of written formalization itself but rather in certain defects in the college's approach to it. Where the purpose of codification has not been clear, so that a governing document has inadvertently become a receptacle for miscellaneous matters of official record, or where a *regulation* concerning a problem has been substituted for a *solution* of the problem, the resulting difficulties seem to the writer not to constitute evidence against the value of documents as such.

Some of the disadvantages of informal patterns, however, do seem inherent in their informality, such as the inevitable lack of certainty as to whether the "unwritten constitution" in effect exists, and whether democratic procedures allegedly observed are, as a matter of course, actually carried out. In support of this opinion it is recalled that the sharpest disagreement between the

116

accounts of policies and procedures as given by junior and senior people occurred in institutions where the rights of junior members were least explicit. The writer does not accept, therefore, without additional evidence, the statement occasionally heard that a college has such a powerful unwritten constitution that written guarantees would be superfluous.

Subject to individual variation in needs among institutions, then, the writer feels that the Academic Bill of Rights and Obligations postulated for purposes of analysis may reasonably be regarded as a generalized charter of matters worthy of being formalized in a written code. This view applies particularly to Principles 1 through 8, relating to appointment, promotion, tenure, salary, and other conditions affecting the teacher's status as an employee; to Principles 9 and 11, relating to academic freedom, sabbatical leave, and assistance in professional development; and to Principles 14, 15, and 16, relating to democracy in the faculty structure and in the relationships among faculty, administration, and trustees.

The writer does not necessarily propose the written embodiment of every specific application of these principles discussed in Chapter II, nor does he suggest any one set of provisions as a model. It would be a simple matter to select from the Comparative Synopsis a composite set of rules, all of which seem well thought out and applicable to their respective situations. In view of the variation in needs among institutions, however, such a composite model as this would have limited value and might even be misleading. If he were asked to draft a set of governing documents for a particular college, concerning the matters covered by this study, he would proceed, on the basic principles already mentioned, to consider such specific provisions as are presented in the Comparative Synopsis and discussed in Chapter II. Each item, however, would be examined in the light of the size, history, and other conditions of the institution, and in consultation with the faculty, administration, and trustees, all of whose understandings and aspirations must be taken into account in determining the form and substance of the documents to be recommended for adoption.

117

The level of authority from which formal statements affecting rights and obligations should be issued is also a question for the individual institution to decide. A given matter may be regulated by provisions of the board of trustees in one college and by those of the faculty in another, depending in each case on the manner in which the codification procedure has been developed.[8] Where the line between the jurisdictions of board and faculty is difficult to draw, the requirement of a joint conference is an excellent solution. This policy was said to work well in the colleges that followed it.

At this time in the world's history, when social and political changes are occurring at an alarming rate, educational institutions are facing ever new responsibilities in helping society to reckon with change and conflict. In meeting the larger and more complex demands that their modern role makes upon them, educational institutions have themselves become larger and more complex, while the rate of turnover in faculty membership has greatly increased. Under these changing conditions it may well be unrealistic to expect traditional forces and unwritten understandings to govern the rights and obligations of people and groups associated in the manifold endeavors of a college or university.

The experience of these eight institutions seems to show that an effective structure of faculty rights and obligations should not be sought in any one principle or device, such as a code on the one hand or the operation of purely implicit forces on the other. It should be sought in the deliberate working out of problems in relationships by whatever resources are available, including not only traditions and habits but also cooperative effort and even mechanical ingenuity, all applied in an atmosphere of determination that each group and each individual shall understand his place in relation to the whole.

[8] As the study has shown, the contents of board- and faculty-legislated codes often do not reflect clearly the division of function between the two bodies. Much board legislation is likely to be initiated by faculty suggestion, even in areas in which authoritative action is reserved to the board.

BIBLIOGRAPHY

REPORTS AND STATEMENTS OF PRINCIPLES
OF THE AMERICAN ASSOCIATION OF
UNIVERSITY PROFESSORS

"Academic Freedom and Tenure: Statements of Principles." AAUP *Bulletin*, 38:116–123, Spring 1952. (Editorial restatements.)

Reports of Committee T, Committee on the Place and Function of Faculties in College and University Government:

1920: "Report of Committee T on the Place and Function of Faculties in University Government and Administration." J. A. Leighton, Chairman. AAUP *Bulletin*, 6:17–47, March 1920. (Reprinted, with additional material from the 1920 study, in the AAUP *Bulletin*, 10:287–368, May 1924.)

1936: "The Place and Function of Faculties in University Government; Report of Progress of Committee T." G. H. Sabine, Chairman. AAUP *Bulletin*, 22:183–190, March 1936.

1937: "The Place and Function of Faculties in University Government; Report of Committee T." G. H. Sabine, Chairman. AAUP *Bulletin*, 23: 220–228, March 1937.

1938: "The Place and Function of Faculties in University and College Government; Report of Committee T." P. W. Ward, Chairman. AAUP *Bulletin*, 24:141–150, February 1938.

1939: "Place and Function of Faculties in College and University Government." P. W. Ward, Chairman. AAUP *Bulletin*, 25:145–150, April 1939.

1940: "Place and Function of Faculties in College and University Government." P. W. Ward, Chairman. AAUP *Bulletin*, 26:171–189, April 1940.

1941: "The Place and Function of Faculties in University and College Government; Report of Committee T." P. W. Ward, Chairman. AAUP *Bulletin*, 27:156–177, April 1941.

1948: "The Role of Faculties in College and University Government." P. W. Ward, Chairman. AAUP *Bulletin*, 34:55–66, Spring 1948.

1953: "The Place and Function of Faculties in College and University Government; Report of Progress." P. W. Ward, Chairman. AAUP *Bulletin*, 39:300–318, Summer 1953.

GENERAL REFERENCES

Adams, J. E., and H. L. Donovan. "Administration and Organization in American Universities." *Peabody Journal of Education*, 22:328–343, May 1945.

American Council on Education. *Louisiana State University, A Survey Report*. Washington, D. C.: The Council, 1940.

Ashbrook, W. A. "The Organization and Activities of Boards Which Control Institutions of Higher Learning." Unpublished Ph.D. Dissertation. Columbus: Ohio State University, 1930. (Abstract in Ohio State University, *Abstracts of Doctors' Dissertations*, 3:1, 1930.)

Association of Governing Boards of State Universities and Allied Institutions. *Proceedings*. N.p.: The Association, 1924.

Beck, H. P. *Men Who Control Our Universities*. New York: King's Crown Press, 1947.

Benjamin, H., ed. *Democracy in the Administration of Higher Education*. Tenth Yearbook of the John Dewey Society. New York: Harper & Brothers, Publishers, 1950.

Bixler, R. W. *Institution-Faculty Relationships in the College of Integrity*. New York: Bureau of Publications, Teachers College, Columbia University, 1939.

Bogert, G. G. "Faculty Participation in American University Government." AAUP *Bulletin*, 31:72–82, Spring 1945.

Burns, N. "Higher Education." *Review of Educational Research*, 22:375–385, October 1952.

Burns, N., ed. *The Administration of Higher Institutions Under Changing Conditions*. Proceedings of the Institute for Administrative Officers of Higher Institutions. Chicago: The University of Chicago Press, 1947.

Burns, N., and C. O. Houle, eds. *The Community Responsibilities of Institutions of Higher Learning*. Proceedings of the Institute for Administrative Officers of Higher Institutions. Chicago: The University of Chicago Press, 1948.

Cattell, J. M., ed. *University Control*. New York: Science Press, 1913.

Chambers, M. M. *The Colleges and the Courts, 1936–40*. New York: The Carnegie Foundation, 1941.

Chambers, M. M. "The Colleges and the Courts in 1946." *Educational Record*, 28:173–189, April 1947.

Chambers, M. M. "Municipal University Business." *College and University Business*, 3:23–24, September 1947.

Childs, J. L. "The Democratic Resolution of Conflicts." H. G. Hullfish, ed. *Educational Freedom in an Age of Anxiety.* Twelfth Yearbook of the John Dewey Society. New York: Harper & Brothers, Publishers, c1953. Pp. 185–205.

Cowley, W. H. "Academic Government." *Educational Forum,* 15:217–229, January 1951.

Cowley, W. H. "The Government and Administration of Higher Education, Whence and Whither?" *Journal of the American Association of Collegiate Registrars,* 22:477–491, July 1947.

Cowley, W. H. "Professional Growth and Academic Freedom." *Journal of Higher Education,* 21:225–236, May 1950.

Cubberley, E. P. *The History of Education.* Boston: Houghton Mifflin Co., 1920.

Eliot, C. W. *University Administration.* Boston: Houghton Mifflin Co., 1908.

Elliott, E. C. "The Board of Control." R. A. Kent, ed. *Higher Education in America.* New York: Ginn and Co., 1930. Pp. 600–632.

Elliott, E. C., and M. M. Chambers. *Charters and Basic Laws of Selected American Colleges and Universities.* New York: The Carnegie Foundation, 1934.

Elliott, E. C., and M. M. Chambers. *The Colleges and the Courts.* New York: Merrymount Press, 1945.

Elliott, E. C., M. M. Chambers, and W. A. Ashbrook. *The Government of Higher Education.* New York: American Book Co., 1935.

Falvey, F. E. *Student Participation in College Administration.* New York: Bureau of Publications, Teachers College, Columbia University, 1952.

Follett, M. P. *Creative Experience.* New York: Longmans, Green and Co., 1925.

Gasset, Ortega y. *Mission of the University.* Princeton, N. J.: Princeton University Press, 1944.

Greenough, W. C. *College Retirement and Insurance Plans.* New York: Columbia University Press, 1948.

Haggerty, M. E. *The Faculty.* Chicago: The University of Chicago Press, 1937.

Hughes, R. M. *A Manual for Trustees of Colleges and Universities.* Ames, Ia.: Collegiate Press, 1945.

Hutchins, R. M. "Freedom of the University." *College and University Business,* 10:19–22, February 1951.

Johnshoy, H. G. "The Government and Administration of Institutions of Higher Education." Unpublished Ed.D. Project Report. New York: Teachers College, Columbia University, 1951.

Keezer, D. M. "The Human Element in College and University Administration." *College and University,* 25:213–232, January 1950.

Kirkpatrick, J. E. *Academic Organization and Control.* Yellow Springs, Ohio: The Antioch Press, 1931.

Kirkpatrick, J. E. *The American College and Its Rulers.* New York: New Republic, 1926.

Kirkpatrick, J. E. *Toryism in American College Government.* Ann Arbor, Mich.: George Wahr, 1923.

121

Knight, E. W. *What College Presidents Say.* Chapel Hill: University of North Carolina Press, 1940.

Leonard, R. J., E. S. Evenden, and F. B. O'Rear. *Survey of Higher Education for the United Lutheran Church in America.* New York: Bureau of Publications, Teachers College, Columbia University, 1929.

Lindsay, E. E., and E. O. Holland. *College and University Administration.* New York: The Macmillan Co., 1930.

MacIver, R. M. "The Freedom to Search for Knowledge." *New York Times Magazine,* April 12, 1953.

McAllister, C. E. *Inside the Campus.* New York: F. H. Revell Co., 1948.

McGrath, E. J. "The Control of Higher Education in America." *Educational Record,* 17:259–272, April 1936.

McVey, F. L., and R. M. Hughes. *Problems of College and University Administration.* Ames: Iowa State College Press, 1952.

Meiklejohn, A. "The Teaching of Intellectual Freedom." AAUP *Bulletin,* 38:10, Spring 1952.

Pattison, M. *Suggestions on Academic Organization, with Specific Reference to Oxford.* Edinburgh: 1868.

Porter, N. *The American Colleges and the American Public.* New Haven, Conn.: Chas. C. Chatfield Co., 1870.

Reeves, F. W., and J. D. Russell. *College Organization and Administration.* Indianapolis, Ind.: Board of Education, Disciples of Christ, 1929.

Reeves, F. W., J. D. Russell, *et al. The Liberal Arts College.* Chicago: The University of Chicago Press, 1932.

Reeves, F. W., F. J. Kelly, J. D. Russell, and G. A. Works. *The Organization and Administration of the University.* (University of Chicago Survey.) Chicago: The University of Chicago Press, 1933.

Reutter, E. E. *The School Administrator and Subversive Activities.* New York: Bureau of Publications, Teachers College, Columbia University, 1951.

Russell, J. D. "Organization and Administration," in section, "Colleges and Universities." *Encyclopedia of Educational Research.* Rev. ed. 1950. Pp. 236–246.

Russell, J. D. "Some Reflections Concerning University Administration." AAUP *Bulletin,* 35:476–489, Autumn 1949.

Russell, J. D., and F. W. Reeves. *Administration.* Chicago: The University of Chicago Press, 1936.

Russell, J. D., ed. *Problems of Faculty Personnel.* Proceedings of the Institute for Administrative Officers of Higher Institutions. Chicago: The University of Chicago Press, 1946.

Scott, D. "Professors Administrant." AAUP *Bulletin,* 28:247–256, April 1942.

Scott, D. "Rationale of Academic Freedom." AAUP *Bulletin,* 36:629–645, Winter 1950.

Shryock, R. H. "The Academic Profession in the United States." AAUP *Bulletin,* 38:32–70, Spring 1952.

Sinclair, U. *The Goose-Step: A Study of American Education.* 4th ed. rev. Pasadena, Calif.: The Author, 1923.

Strayer, G. D., and A. J. Klein. *Report of a Survey of the Institutions of Higher Learning in the State of Iowa.* Submitted to the State Board of Education of Iowa, 1950.

Teachers College, Columbia University. *Statutes and By-Laws and Other Official Documents.* New York: The College, 1950.

Tead, O. *The Art of Administration.* New York: McGraw-Hill Book Co., 1951.

Tead, O. "Faculty-Administration Relationships in the Colleges of New York: Ten-Year Appraisal." AAUP *Bulletin,* 34:67–78, March 1948.

Tead, O. "The Place and Functions of the Faculty in College Government." AAUP *Bulletin,* 25:163–168, April 1939.

Tead, O. *Trustees, Teachers, Students: Their Role in Higher Education.* Salt Lake City: University of Utah Press, 1951.

Thompson, A. R. "The Professor and the Governing Board." AAUP *Bulletin,* 35:678–687, Winter 1949.

Thwing, C. F. *A History of Higher Education in America.* New York: D. Appleton & Co., 1906.

Trecker, H. B. *Group Process in Administration.* 2nd ed. rev. New York: Woman's Press, 1950.

U. S. Office of Education. "Control of Higher Education in Illinois." *Higher Education,* March 1, 1951, p. 145.

U. S. Office of Education. *Education Directory, 1952–53.* Pt. 3: "Higher Education." Washington, D. C.: Government Printing Office, 1952.

U. S. Office of Education. *Surveys of Higher Education in the United States, 1937–49.* Circular No. 257. Washington, D. C.: Government Printing Office, May 1949.

Veblen, T. *Higher Learning in America: A Memorandum on the Conduct of Universities by Business Men.* New York: Huebsch, 1918.

Verhaalen, R. J. "Legislation and Higher Education: Laws and By-Laws Affecting the Government of Public Institutions of Higher Learning." Unpublished Ph.D. Dissertation. Laramie: University of Wyoming, 1948. (Digest in University of Wyoming, *Bureau of Educational Research and Service Bulletin,* 8, no. 2 [entire issue], 1948.)

Wold, L. "Legal Separation of Function in University Organization." *Quarterly Journal of the University of North Dakota,* 10:61–81, October 1921.

Wilson, Logan. *The Academic Man.* London, New York: Oxford University Press, 1942.

Woodburne, L. S. *Faculty Personnel Policies in Higher Education.* New York: Harper & Brothers, Publishers, 1950.

Woodburne, L. S., and N. P. Meade. *An Appraisal of the Faculty Organization By-Laws Governing the College of the City of New York.* New York: The Board of Higher Education, September 1, 1950.

123

PROVISIONS AND PRACTICES

IN THE EIGHT COLLEGES

The Comparative Synopsis contains the principal data on whic' this book is based. It is designed for use either as a reference in itself c as an aid to reading the text.

The rights and obligations discussed in the Comparative Synopsis mak up the Academic Bill of Rights and Obligations presented in Chapter I Because this study is concerned with the extent to which faculty right and obligations are officially recognized in each of the eight institution: the description of each provision or practice is followed by a reference i (1) the group on whose authority the provision or practice rests; (2) th status of the provision or practice; (3) the name of the document cor taining the provision, if it is committed to writing. For example, "FAC. REC (*Fac. Info.*)" refers to an official, written rule promulgated by the facult and contained in *Information for Members of the Faculty,* a document c Haverford College. The authority, the status, and the document containin the written statement of a provision may, of course, all be conveyed in single phrase, such as *B-L of Trus.,* which refers to a regulation of the go' erning board recorded in its by-laws.

TABLE OF ABBREVIATIONS

NOTE: Wherever abbreviations for two or more governing author ties appear in the Comparative Synopsis separated by hyphens, th provision or practice in question appears to rest on joint authorit' For example, "TRUS.-FAC. POL." refers to a policy for which trustee and faculty are jointly responsible.

AAUP–AAC *Principles,* the 1940 "Statement of Principles on Academic Freedom and Tenure," endorsed by the American Association of University Professors, the Association of American Colleges, and several other educational associations ("Academic Freedom and Tenure: Statements of Principles," AAUP *Bulletin,* 38:116, Spring 1952)

Ac. Coun., Academic Council (Wesleyan)

Ac. Stat., *Academic Statute* (in *Governance of Vassar College*)

adm., administration (president and central administrative organization)

Adv. Comm., Advisory Committee:
Mount Holyoke—Advisory Committee on Appointments, Reappointments, and Promotions
Sarah Lawrence—Advisory Committee on Appointments
Vassar—Advisory Committee
Wesleyan—Advisory Committee (of Academic Council)

Adv. Coun., Advisory Council (President's Advisory Council, Colleges of the Seneca)

B-L, *By-Laws* (of governing board or of faculty, as indicated)

bull., bulletin

CREF, College Retirement Equities Fund

corp., corporation

fac., faculty

Fac. Info., *Information for Members of the Faculty* (Haverford)

Fac. Regs., *Faculty Regulations* (Swarthmore)

Hdbk., *Handbook:*
Colgate—*Faculty Handbook*
Mount Holyoke—*Handbook of Faculty Legislation and Related Information*

interp., interpretation, interpreted

mgrs., board of managers (governing board—Haverford, Swarthmore)

pol., policy (without regard to whether it is statutory or formally stated)

prac., practice (what is actually done, with or without reference to a consciously formulated policy or to tradition or usage)

Prins., *Principles Governing the Relations of Trustees and Faculty* (in *Governance of Vassar College*)

pub., published

q-stat., quasi-statutory (regarded as having force similar to that of a statute, though not formally stated by the trustees or legally traceable to the authority vested in the trustees)

reg., regulation (an official rule, whether written or not)

stud., student government association

TIAA, Teachers Insurance and Annuity Association of America

trus., board of trustees

unwr., unwritten (at least, not found in any document having either general circulation or official recognition)

PART I: RIGHTS AND OBLIGATIONS RELATING TO PER SONAL AND PROFESSIONAL STATUS

Principle 1: The right and the obligation to be governed by clear an mutually binding terms of appointment.

1-a. Formalization of appointment by contract or other written com mitment.

COLGATE. Terms and conditions of every appointment are to be ii writing and in possession of both college and appointee before an appoint ment is made.—TRUS. REG. (*Hdbk.*)

HAVERFORD. Terms and conditions of every appointment are to bi in writing and in possession of both president and appointee.—MGRS. REG (*Fac. Info.*)

HOBART. "Written notification of appointment to the individual by th President . . ." is implied policy.—*B-L of Trus.*[1] (Writer's interp.; als adm. prac.) Answer in writing is requested. Exchange of letters is re garded as a contract.—ADM. PRAC. (Unwr.)

MOUNT HOLYOKE. For professorial ranks, letter from presiden states length of appointment, salary for first year, and whether or not ap pointment is probationary. In connection with the last-named point, lette states that college reserves right to make special agreements but that i endorses in general the AAUP–AAC *Principles* on academic freedom an tenure. Certain of terms of appointment, including provisions with respec to insurance and TIAA, are also mentioned. Written acknowledgmer required within fourteen days.—TRUS.-ADM. POL. (*Hdbk.*)

SARAH LAWRENCE. Contract letter from president states length c appointment, salary, and retirement age; specifies that unless appointmei is part-time, outside employment "which might be detrimental to fu service to the College" shall not be undertaken, the administration being th judge; and specifies that no other terms have been agreed on except thos "explicitly stated above." Acknowledgment required.—ADM. PRAC. (Unwr.

SWARTHMORE. Letter of appointment sent to each appointee b president.—ADM. PRAC. (Unwr.)

VASSAR. Terms of employment must be expressed in contract, whic "shall constitute the sole basis of the individual's service in the college."- TRUS. REG. (*Prins.*)

[1] The full title of the Hobart document referred to throughout the Comparativ Synopsis as "*B-L of Trus.*" is *By-Laws of the Colleges of the Seneca.*

WESLEYAN. Notice of appointment, reappointment, promotion, and
ermination of appointment given in writing by president. Acknowledg-
1ent required. Oral assurances not considered binding.—ADM. PRAC. (B-L
f Ac. Coun.; Q-stat.)

**'rinciple 2: The right to an understanding of the conditions governing
duration of appointment and chances for promotion.**

-a. *Statement of qualifications for appointment and promotion to
each rank.*

COLGATE. General description given of qualifications for appointment
r promotion to each academic rank. The only specific condition is that,
or professorial ranks, doctorate or equivalent evidence of "maturity and
ttainment in the field of scholarship" is normally expected. Full professor-
hip "should never be granted as a reward of seniority" or for "usefulness
1 administration."—TRUS. REG. (Hdbk.)

HAVERFORD. No official provisions.

HOBART. Requirement of doctorate for promotion beyond instructor-
hip is announced policy, though exceptions are made in certain fields in
vhich doctorate is not considered a scholarly necessity. Also, new faculty
1ember is sometimes appointed to assistant professorship prior to his com-
letion of doctorate.—ADM.-ADV. COUN. POL. (Unwr.)

MOUNT HOLYOKE. General statement of qualifications for promotion
1entions productive scholarship or creative work, outstanding ability in
eaching, and service to college, department, and community. Length of
ervice explicitly excluded as primary reason for promotion.—TRUS.-ADM.-
DV. COMM. POL. (Hdbk.)

SARAH LAWRENCE. No academic ranks exist; hence, following state-
1ent applies only to criteria for appointment and reappointment: Faculty
must agree on certain basic principles. . . . We should not have faculty
1embers who believe that mastery of material is all that counts, or . . .
ho believe that mastery of material is a minor or irrelevant factor in de-
elopment. . . ."—TRUS.-FAC. POL. ("Statement of Principles and Pro-
edures," report by faculty Planning Committee, accepted by trustees;
ence, Q-stat.)

SWARTHMORE. No official provisions.

VASSAR. Description given of qualifications for appointment or promo-
on to each academic rank. Ph.D. or equivalent is normally expected for
ınk of instructor.—TRUS. REG. (Ac. Stat.) Ph.D. or equivalent is definite
equirement for professorial rank.—ADV. COMM. POL. (Unwr.)

127

WESLEYAN. Personal and professional qualities to be considered ir judging candidate for appointment or promotion officially stated in genera way. No specific reference made to qualifications for each rank,—*B-L o) Ac. Coun.* (Q-stat.)

2-b. Statement of policies governing duration of appointment.

COLGATE. No official provisions, except statement that it shall be gen- eral policy not to continue appointment of instructors beyond sixth year.— TRUS. REG. (*Hdbk.*) One-year appointments general for instructors.— ADM. PRAC. (Unwr.)

HAVERFORD. Usual practice is as follows: Instructor, one year for initial appointment—second appointment *may* be for two years; assistant professor, three years; associate professor, five years (note that continuou: tenure is acquired in seven years); professor, normally continuous tenure.— MGRS.-ADM. PRAC. (Unwr.) Policy on length of term appointment is un written; granting of continuous tenure is statutory (see Items 4-*b* and 4-*c*)
Exception: Although professors normally have continuous tenure, proba tionary period may be specified in initial appointment (see Item 4-*c*).— MGRS. REG. (*Fac. Info.*)

HOBART. Instructor, one year; assistant professor, two years; associate professor, indefinite length, continuous tenure becoming automatic if ap pointment is not terminated in three years; professor, same as for associate professor.—*B-L of Trus.*
Exceptions: (1) Associate professor or professor may be given term ap pointment instead of arrangement described above.—*B-L of Trus.* (2) In structor may be given two-year appointment the second time (first reap pointment). (3) Instructors not kept without promotion after six years except under unusual circumstances.—TRUS.-ADM. PRAC. (Unwr.)

MOUNT HOLYOKE. Assistant, one year; instructor, one year; assistant professor, three years (first term probationary); associate professor, three years for first appointment and five years for subsequent appointments professor, four years for first appointment and continuous tenure for second appointment; lecturer (various ranks), usually temporary or part-time.— TRUS.-ADM. POL. (*Hdbk.*)

SARAH LAWRENCE. No academic ranks exist; hence, following regula tions apply to all faculty members: First appointment, normally two years second appointment, normally two years; third and subsequent appoint ments, normally four years.—ADM.-FAC. REG. (*Fac. B-L*)
Additional provisions: (1) If no four-year contract is to be given afte two two-year terms, appointee is given option of one additional year a college. (2) If faculty member has had two one-year appointments as sub stitute teacher, followed by one two-year appointment, he is normally giver four-year appointment.—ADM.-FAC. REG. (*Fac. B-L*)

128

SWARTHMORE. Instructor, one year; assistant professor, three years; associate professor, five years; professor, indefinite term.—MGRS.-FAC. REG. ("Joint Resolution Concerning Faculty Tenure," March 11, 1924, pub. separately; also in *Fac. Regs.*)

Reservations: (1) In any rank, initial probationary appointment may be or one or two years. (2) Appointments may be less than one year in case f emergency—e.g., filling in for teacher on leave, and the like.—MGRS.-AC. REG. ("Joint Resolution Concerning Faculty Tenure"; also in *Fac. egs.*)

VASSAR. Instructor, one year (except at top salary, in which case two ears); assistant professor, two years for first appointment and three years or second appointment; associate professor, three years each for first and second appointments and continuous tenure after six years; professor, five ears for first appointment and continuous tenure after five years as associate professor or professor.—TRUS. REG. (*Ac. Stat.*)

Exception: Under special circumstances, appointment may be for shorter erm than here specified.—TRUS. REG. (*Ac. Stat.*)

WESLEYAN. Instructor, two years [2] (total service in rank not to exceed four years); assistant professor, not more than two years (total service as assistant professor and instructor not to exceed seven years); associate rofessor, each appointment not more than three years (appointment made nly in anticipation of ultimate promotion to professorship).—TRUS. POL. B-L *of Ac. Coun.;* Q-stat.) Professor, continuous tenure.—TRUS.-ADM. POL. Unwr.) Total period of associate professorship customarily six years.—OM. PRAC. (Unwr.)

rinciple 3: The right to fair and objective processes in matters of reappointment, promotion, and increase in salary.

-a. Principal processes recognized in effecting an appointment or reappointment.[3]

COLGATE. Steps required by statute: President recommends; board ppoints.—*Charter.* No other consultations officially required.

Other policies and practices: President consults with faculty members, enior in rank to person under consideration, whose opinions are especially ertinent.—ADM. PRAC. (Unwr.) In general, department chairman's rec-

[2] *By-Laws of the Academic Council* state that appointments are normally for ie year; however, policy has changed to two years.

[3] Items 3-*a* and 3-*b* are concerned with the rights and obligations of the faculty ember with respect to his own appointment; Item 14-*b* deals with his rights and ligations with respect to action affecting his colleagues. Since the data relating these two complementary topics are in large part the same, they are given just ice, under Principle 3, and reference is made to this presentation elsewhere as propriate.

129

ommendation is primary consideration. President's role in decision is mos likely to be crucial when positions of higher responsibility are involved.— ADM. PRAC. (Unwr.)

HAVERFORD. Steps required by statute: No official provisions, excep general statement that employment of teachers is entrusted to board o managers.—*Charter.*

Other policies and practices: For initial appointment, president recom mends after consultation with department chairman and committee of divi sional representatives. For important appointments, *ad hoc* committees ar frequently designated by president. Committee members and others con sulted include faculty members, senior to person under consideration, wh may have important interest in appointment or who may be expected t offer impartial judgment needed.—ADM. PRAC. (Unwr.) On reappoint ments, president confers with Administrative Committee (vice-president dean, and the two faculty representatives on the board), though consulta tive steps described above for initial appointments may also be followe prior to decision on reappointments.—ADM. PRAC. (Unwr.)

HOBART. Steps required by statute: Trustees have power to appoin faculty members.—*Charter.* President nominates; board appoints.—*B-L o Trus.* No other consultations officially required.

Other policies and practices: President consults with Advisory Counci (four administrative officers *ex officio* and three professors elected by fac ulty). Decision usually made at this stage, by consensus. President con sults department chairman involved, whose recommendation is an impor tant factor in all cases and principal consideration in some. Informal con sultation with other faculty members whose views are especially pertinen Considerable informal but established procedure carried out before forma action.—ADM.-ADV. COUN. PRAC. (Unwr.)

MOUNT HOLYOKE. Steps required by statute: Department chairma must be consulted. Faculty Advisory Committee on Appointments, Reap pointments, and Promotions (elected) must be consulted, except in case of instructors who have served less than three years.[4]—*B-L of Trus.*

Other policies and practices: Informal consultations carried on by pres dent and Advisory Committee with faculty members.—ADM. PRAC. (Unwr. Trustee Committee on Education *may* be asked by president to confer wit Advisory Committee before he formally recommends.—*B-L of Trus.* (A tually, this is not generally done.) In general, department chairman's re ommendation is deciding factor in less important appointments, Advisor Committee's decision in the more important. President rarely reverse recommendation of Advisory Committee. In any case, recommendations c Advisory Committee always transmitted to board by president.—ADM. PRA (Unwr.)

[4] I.e., Advisory Committee is consulted on instructors only when tenure is i prospect.—ADM. PRAC. (Intent of *B-L of Trus.*)

SARAH LAWRENCE. Steps required by statute: President nominates and executes contracts of appointment.—*B-L of Trus.*

Other policies and practices: President consults with Advisory Committee on Appointments (three faculty-elected members plus dean *ex officio*).[5] —ADM.-FAC. POL. (*Fac. B-L*) Actually, president and Advisory Committee work as committee of five, consulting widely among faculty and generally reaching decisions by consensus.—ADM.-FAC. PRAC. (Unwr.)

SWARTHMORE. Steps required by statute: Employment of "professors and other officers" entrusted to board of managers.—*Charter.* President recommends; board appoints.—*B-L of Corp.* No other consultations officially required.

Other policies and practices: President consults informally the faculty members whose views are especially pertinent. Department chairman is principal adviser.—ADM. PRAC. (Unwr.) For initial appointment of general interest to faculty, there is likely to be, in addition, an advisory *ad hoc* committee appointed by president (Item 15-*e* explains manner of constituting committee).—ADM.-FAC. PRAC. (Unwr.)

VASSAR. Steps required by statute: No faculty appointment or removal can be effected except by majority vote of all trustees.—*Charter.* Department members of higher rank than candidate nominate by ballot.— FAC. REG. (*Ac. Stat.*) President consults Advisory Committee (three professors elected by faculty). President recommends to board (via trustee Committee on Faculty and Studies).—TRUS. REG. (*Ac. Stat.*)

Other policies and practices: Department chairman's recommendation is important factor in all cases.—ADM.-ADV. COMM. PRAC. (Unwr.) Wide informal consultation within department before nominations are made.— FAC. PRAC. (Unwr.)

WESLEYAN. Steps required by statute: President must seek approval of nominations by Academic Council (composed, in effect, of president, dean of the faculty, and full professors) before presenting them to board of trustees. President must present nominations of Academic Council to trustees whether he endorses them or not. Before recommending contrary to Academic Council, president must confer with trustee Committee on Faculty and Curriculum. Trustees may appoint without president's nomination after rejecting his first three candidates.—*B-L of Trus.* Overriding of president or Academic Council, as provided for above, does not occur in practice.

Other policies and practices: Department's recommendation (i.e., recommendation of senior members of department—see Item 14-*a*) is usually main consideration.—ADM.-AC. COUN. PRAC. (Unwr.) President "may" confer with Advisory Committee (professors elected by Academic Council)

---

[5] Appointments of business administration officers are not considered by the Advisory Committee, even though such officers are members of the "general faculty."—ADM.-FAC. POL. (*Fac. B-L*)

131

before presenting his nominations to Academic Council.—*B-L of Ac. Coun.* (Q-stat.) In effect, however, he *must* do so.—ADM.-AC. COUN. PRAC. (Unwr.) President and Advisory Committee generally formulate decision, which is then approved by Academic Council, president (officially), trustee Committee on Faculty and Curriculum, and trustees, in that order.— TRUS.-ADM.-AC. COUN. PRAC. (Unwr.)

3-*b*. *Principal processes recognized in effecting a promotion or increase in salary.*

COLGATE. Steps required by statute: Same as for reappointment. Other policies and practices: Same as for reappointment, except that consultation of faculty members does not include matters of individual salary. "Promotions are determined by the combined judgment of the departmental chairman, the divisional director, the Dean of the Faculty, and the President, with the approval of the Board of Trustees."—ADM. POL. AND PRAC. (*Hdbk.*)

HAVERFORD. For promotion, same procedures as for reappointment. For salary increase, consultation only at discretion of president. Administrative Committee as such is not consulted.—ADM. PRAC. (Unwr.)

HOBART. Same procedures as for reappointment, except that Advisory Council does not participate in determining salary increases of full professors. In practice, promotions do not occur without approval of Advisory Council.—ADM.-ADV. COUN. PRAC. (Unwr.)

MOUNT HOLYOKE. Same procedures as for reappointment, except that Advisory Committee is not consulted on salary increases as such.

SARAH LAWRENCE. No academic ranks; hence, question of promotion not applicable. Advisory Committee on Appointments makes recommendations on salary increases. Criteria considered are length of service, initial salary, past rate of increase, comparability with other salaries, and effectiveness in position.—ADM.-FAC. POL. ("Statement of Principles and Procedures," report by faculty Planning Committee, accepted by trustees; hence, Q-stat.)

SWARTHMORE. Same procedures as for reappointment.

VASSAR. In general, same procedures as for reappointment. At least once in five years Advisory Committee considers promotion of associate professors at maximum salary for their rank and advancement in salary of full professors below maximum salary.—TRUS.-FAC. REG. (*Ac. Stat.*)

WESLEYAN. Same procedures as for appointment, except that Academic Council and departments are not consulted on questions of salary raises as such.

132

Principle 4: The right to achieve continuous tenure after sufficient time to prove oneself.[6]

4-a. Explicit recognition of continuous tenure as a principle.

COLGATE. Principles of tenure officially adopted by trustees and published in *Faculty Handbook* by administration.—TRUS. REG. (*Hdbk.*)

HAVERFORD. Principles of tenure officially adopted and published. Adapted from AAUP–AAC *Principles.*—MGRS. REG. (*Fac. Info.*)

HOBART. Principles of tenure officially adopted by trustees and published.—*B-L of Trus.* Trustee-administration policy actually followed, however, goes beyond formal by-laws, extending continuous tenure to lower two ranks on basis of AAUP–AAC *Principles.* (Policy is referred to at Hobart as "de facto tenure.")—TRUS.-ADM. POL. (Unwr.; Q-stat.)

MOUNT HOLYOKE. AAUP–AAC *Principles* said to be followed in general, though college reserves right to make special agreements.—TRUS.-ADM. POL. (*Hdbk.;* also in letter of appointment.)

SARAH LAWRENCE. No official provisions. Continuous tenure considered to be in effect, however, since presumption of permanency is implicit in granting of second four-year appointment or first four-year appointment extending beyond seventh year of service. Continuous tenure, therefore, is approximately the same as set forth in AAUP–AAC *Principles.* (See Item 2-*b* regarding sequence of term appointments.)

SWARTHMORE. Professors appointed for "indefinite term."—MGRS. REG. ("Joint Resolution Concerning Faculty Tenure"; also in *Fac. Regs.*) No other published legislation. AAUP–AAC *Principles* represent recognized policy, except that probationary time is not transferable from another institution.—MGRS.-ADM. POL. (Unwr.)

VASSAR. Principles of tenure officially adopted by trustees and published.—TRUS. REG. (*Ac. Stat.*)

WESLEYAN. No published legislation. Continuous tenure is by traditional understanding in effect for all full professors, and for associate professors unless otherwise stated in letter of appointment.—TRUS.-ADM.-FAC. PRAC. (Unwr.)

[6] *Continuous tenure* is defined as expectation of continuous appointment until retirement, to be terminated only under conditions fully covered by mutually understood provisions.

4-b. Designation of ranks that, under the recognized rules, may achieve continuous tenure.[7]

COLGATE. Professors
Associate professors
Assistant professors
Instructors not excluded by formal rule, but it is contrary to administrative policy to recommend reappointment to rank of instructor after six years of service.—TRUS. REG. (*Hdbk.*) Reservations exist regarding tenure for certain groups of appointees (see Item 4-*e*).

HAVERFORD. Professors
Associate professors
Assistant professors (by special action)
Instructors (by special action)
For assistant professors and instructors, continuous tenure awarded by special action only, on individual basis; general policy is not to grant tenure to members of these ranks under forty years of age.—MGRS. POL. (*Fac. Info.*)

HOBART. Professors
Associate professors
Assistant professors
Instructors
Few instructors kept long enough to meet probationary time requirement (see Item 2-*b*).—TRUS.-ADM. POL. (Unwr.) This designation of ranks eligible to achieve continuous tenure is partly statutory and partly unwritten policy (see Item 4-*a*).

MOUNT HOLYOKE. Professors
Associate professors
Assistant professors
Instructors
Appointees usually not kept as instructors long enough to meet probationary time requirement.—TRUS.-ADM. POL. (Unwr.)

SARAH LAWRENCE. All teaching faculty members, to extent of their regular teaching load, except those primarily administrative officers.—ADM.-FAC. POL. (Unwr.; writer's interp.)

SWARTHMORE. Professors
Associate professors
Assistant professors

[7] Table 2 (pp. 28–29) shows the number and percentage of faculty members in each rank who actually *do* have continuous tenure. The following designation of ranks *eligible* to achieve continuous tenure is the writer's interpretation of the various policies and procedures affecting this matter in each institution.

134

Instructors in general not recommended for reappointment to same rank after six years.—ADM. PRAC. (Unwr.)

VASSAR. Professors
    Associate professors
      —TRUS. REG. (*Ac. Stat.*)

WESLEYAN. Professors
    Associate professors
    Assistant professors (special circumstances only)
      —ADM.-AC. COUN. POL. (Unwr.; writer's interp.)
Other ranks excluded by policy of limiting time of service in rank (see Item 2-*b*).

4-c. Provisions governing length of probationary period preceding continuous tenure.

COLGATE. Maximum, seven years, first three of which are transferable from appointment at another institution. For higher ranks, period is shorter: five years as associate professor or four years as professor. Period also shorter for new appointee who has been on tenure elsewhere: maximum, two years, though exception may be made in contract. President may reduce length of probationary period in specific cases, with approval of Executive Committee of board.—TRUS. REG. (*Hdbk.*)

HAVERFORD. Seven years, if granted below rank of professor. No probationary period for professors unless first appointment at college is stipulated in contract to be probationary.—MGRS. REG. (*Fac. Info.*)

HOBART. Maximum, six years below associate professor.—TRUS.-ADM. POL. (Unwr.; Q-stat.) Shorter for associate professors and professors: in effect three years, though exception may be made in contract by granting only term appointment.—*B-L of Trus.* Period may be shorter, in any given instance, than indicated herein, depending on sequence of term appointments, since term appointment may carry past end of probationary period.—WRITER'S INTERP.

MOUNT HOLYOKE. Maximum, seven years, first three of which are transferable from appointment at another institution (implied by endorsement of AAUP–AAC *Principles*).—TRUS.-ADM. POL. (*Hdbk.*) Period shorter, in effect, for professorial ranks, because term appointment may carry past end of probationary period. Hence, effective probationary periods are six years for assistant professor; three to six years for associate professor; four years for professor.—WRITER'S INTERP.

SARAH LAWRENCE. No explicit probationary period, since tenure is not formally recognized. Four years, in effect, constitute probationary period in most cases, since sequence of contracts is two years, two years, and four years, third contract carrying past seventh year of service.—TRUS.-ADM. POL. (Unwr.)

SWARTHMORE. Maximum, six years; in effect, anyone appointed past sixth year has continuous tenure.—MGRS.-ADM. POL. (Unwr.) Period may be shortened, since term appointment may carry past end of probationary period, amount depending on sequence of appointments preceding that in which tenure is achieved.—WRITER'S INTERP.

VASSAR. Six years as associate professor; five years as professor or as associate professor and professor.—TRUS.-FAC. REG. (*Ac. Stat.;* writer's interp.)

WESLEYAN. No probationary period specified, except in individual appointments. In practice, however, maximum probationary period of seven years is observed.—TRUS.-ADM. PRAC. (Unwr.)

4-d. *Limitation of right of continuous tenure: Circumstances of the institution under which tenure may become invalid.*[8]

COLGATE. (1) Reorganization of curriculum by faculty; (2) financial exigency (extraordinary circumstances).—TRUS. REG. (*Hdbk.*)

HAVERFORD. (1) Revision of curriculum, permanent or protracted; (2) financial exigency. In case of revision of curriculum, every effort is to be made first to adjust situation through shifts in teaching assignments. Action may be taken only after consultation with faculty representatives chosen for the purpose by faculty.—MGRS. REG. (*Fac. Info.*)

HOBART. (1) Financial exigency; (2) necessary change in educational policy. Action under either of these conditions, however, is subject to same due process as dismissal (see Items 6-*c* through 6-*f*).—B-L of *Trus.*

MOUNT HOLYOKE. No official provisions, except that endorsement is made of AAUP–AAC *Principles,* by which "financial exigencies" may be recognized as valid grounds for termination of tenure.—TRUS.-ADM. POL. (*Hdbk.;* also in letter of appointment.)

SARAH LAWRENCE. No official provisions. AAUP–AAC *Principles* would tend to be followed.—ADM.-FAC. POL. (Unwr.)

SWARTHMORE. No explicit official provisions. AAUP–AAC *Principles* would presumably apply, since they constitute the conscious tenure policy, though not formalized as such.—ADM. POL. (Unwr.; writer's interp.)

[8] For invalidation of tenure chargeable to the appointee rather than conditions of the institution, see Item 6-*b*.

136

VASSAR. Continuous tenure conditional upon continuance in curriculum of full-time work for which appointee is qualified. If, for five years, less than full-time work is available, trustees may modify or terminate appointment on recommendation of Advisory Committee.—TRUS. REG. (*Ac. Stat.*)

WESLEYAN. No official provisions. Reservation sometimes made in letter of appointment by phrase "circumstances permitting" or equivalent wording. AAUP–AAC *Principles* said to govern.—ADM. POL. (Unwr.)

4-e. Other qualifications and interpretations relating to the right of continuous tenure.

COLGATE. Tenure rules do not apply to division of physical education, where tenure is awarded only at discretion of trustees. Tenure rules apply only to people concerned primarily with instruction (e.g., not to administrators who may have only minor concern with educational program). Notification of continuous tenure given in writing. Future amendments of tenure legislation may not deprive anyone of tenure earned under present conditions.—TRUS. REG. (*Hdbk.*)

HAVERFORD. Time on sabbatical leave may be counted as probationary time served. Full-time service of a visiting teacher of any rank may be counted as probationary time served. Appointee's seven probationary years need not be consecutive.—MGRS. REG. (*Fac. Info.*)

HOBART. Any interruption of probationary service subtracted from total credited.—TRUS.-ADM. PRAC. (Unwr.)

MOUNT HOLYOKE. For professorial ranks, intent of college to extend benefits of continuous tenure goes beyond formal statement of policy (referred to in Item 4-*a*). Assistant professor's first term (three years) explicitly probationary (TRUS.-ADM. POL. [*Hdbk.*]); otherwise, presumption is that members of top three ranks will earn continuous tenure.—TRUS.-ADM. POL. (Unwr.)

SARAH LAWRENCE. Continuous tenure limited for part-time teachers; if faculty member reduces his teaching time for more than two years, he cannot expect to be employed thereafter for greater number of days per week than his decreased schedule.—ADM.-FAC. REG. (*Fac. B-L*)

SWARTHMORE. Time on sabbatical leave may be counted as probationary time served.—ADM. POL. (Unwr.)

VASSAR. Time on leave with faculty fellowship may be counted as probationary time served.—TRUS. REG. (*Ac. Stat.*)

137

WESLEYAN. Time on leave of absence may be counted as probationary time served, subject to exception by written agreement; for example, voluntary wartime leaves would be excluded by written understanding from counting as probationary time served.—*B-L of Ac. Coun.* (Q-stat.) Drafted men assured of one-year appointment or completion of their current appointment upon honorable separation from armed services. —TRUS. REG. (By resolution; also pub. in *B-L of Ac. Coun.*)

Principle 5: The right to advance notice of non-reappointment or dismissal,[9] and the obligation to give advance notice of voluntary resignation.

5-a. Provisions for advance notice of non-reappointment.

COLGATE. Instructors to be informed at least by March 1 of year of termination, earlier if possible.—TRUS. REG. (*Hdbk.*)

HAVERFORD. December notification for instructors and assistant professors.—MGRS.-ADM. PRAC. (Unwr.) For termination of service of faculty member with tenure, because of change in academic program: two years' notice with full salary.—MGRS. REG. (*Fac. Info.*)

HOBART. Instructors to be notified six months before termination of service; assistant professors, one year; associate professors and professors not on continuous tenure,[10] one year.—*B-L of Trus.* When continuous tenure is in question, instructors, insofar as possible, are informed of their prospects for reappointment more than one year before end of probationary period.— ADM. PRAC. (Unwr.)

MOUNT HOLYOKE. One year's notice before end of probationary period preceding granting of continuous tenure.—TRUS.-ADM. POL. (*Hdbk.*)

SARAH LAWRENCE. For non-reappointment after second year, teacher to be notified by December of that year. For non-reappointment after four-year contract, eighteen months' notice in effect required (see Item 2-*b*).— ADM.-FAC. REG. (*Fac. B-L*)

SWARTHMORE. Notice of non-reappointment to be given three months before end of academic year, except for assistant professors, associate professors, and professors with more than three years of service, who are to

[9] *Dismissal*, unless otherwise indicated, is assumed to mean termination of service despite protection of a term appointment or continuous tenure, and for reasons chargeable to the appointee. For distinctions to be made among the various circumstances of separation, see Table 3 (p. 34).

[10] Associate professors and professors may be on indefinite appointment without having continuous tenure (see Item 2-*b*).

be notified one year before termination of service.—MGRS.-FAC. REG. ("Joint Resolution Concerning Faculty Tenure"; also in *Fac. Regs.*)

VASSAR. Notice of non-reappointment to be given by March 1 for one-year appointments or instructors on two-year appointments; by December 1 for assistant professors; by July 1 of preceding year for associate professors and professors.—TRUS. REG. (*Ac. Stat.*) Department must inform teacher of his prospects for retention or promotion in final year of appointment in which he reaches maximum salary for rank (if instructor or assistant professor) or in final year of second appointment (if associate professor).—TRUS.-FAC. REG. (*Ac. Stat.*)

WESLEYAN. Above rank of instructor, one year's notice is recognized principle.—*B-L of Ac. Coun.* (Q-stat.) One year's notice given to instructors whenever possible.—ADM.-AC. COUN. PRAC. (Unwr.) Academic Council must act by December 15 on all appointments expiring at end of academic year.—*B-L of Ac. Coun.* (Q-stat.) This action is not final but tends to carry official force.

5-b. *Requirements of appointee regarding notice of resignation.*

COLGATE. Professors and associate professors to give at least four months' notice; assistant professors and instructors, three months', but varying with circumstances. Provisions include procedures for dealing with offers of appointment or approaches to such offers from other institutions.—TRUS. REG. (*Hdbk.;* same as in AAUP "Statement Concerning Resignations," 1929.) Resignations to be tendered by March 1; not later than June 1.—ADM. REG. (*Hdbk.*)

HAVERFORD. No official provisions.

HOBART. Instructors to give six months' notice; professorial ranks, one year's notice.—*B-L of Trus.* (Writer's interp.) In practice, resignations usually accepted when offered.—ADM. PRAC. (Unwr.)

MOUNT HOLYOKE. No official provisions.

SARAH LAWRENCE. No official provisions.

SWARTHMORE. "Reasonable time for the College to make necessary readjustments."—MGRS.-FAC. REG. ("Joint Resolution Concerning Faculty Tenure"; also in *Fac. Regs.*)

VASSAR. Three months' notice usually sufficient if termination is by mutual consent.—TRUS. REG. (*Ac. Stat.*)

139

WESLEYAN. Notice by March 15 requested. Recommendation of release from term appointment to be given only if it will not cause serious embarrassment to institution.—*B-L of Ac. Coun.* (Q-stat.) In practice, release always given when requested.

5-c. Specification of interval required for dismissal to take effect.

COLGATE. No official provisions. Note, however, salary settlement in case of dismissal (Item 6-g).

HAVERFORD. No official provisions. Note, however, salary settlement in case of dismissal (Item 6-g).

HOBART. No official provisions.

MOUNT HOLYOKE. No official provisions. Note, however, salary settlement in case of dismissal (Item 6-g).

SARAH LAWRENCE. No official provisions.

SWARTHMORE. Same notice required as for non-reappointment. In case of "grave moral delinquency," period of notice does not apply.—MGRS.-FAC. REG. ("Joint Resolution Concerning Faculty Tenure"; writer's interp.)

VASSAR. Dismissal does not take effect for at least one semester after decision, except when it is for immorality, treason, or gross neglect of duty.—TRUS.-FAC. REG. (*Ac. Stat.*)

WESLEYAN. No official provisions.

Principle 6: The right to some "due process" to assure fairness in case of non-reappointment or dismissal.

6-a. Processes designed to assure fairness in decision of non-reappointment.

COLGATE. No official provisions.

HAVERFORD. No official provisions.

HOBART. No explicit official provisions. Actually, Advisory Council accepts responsibility for decisions.—ADM.-ADV. COUN. PRAC. (Unwr.)

MOUNT HOLYOKE. No explicit official provisions. Right to take up subject with president or Advisory Committee on Appointments, Reappoint-

140

ments, and Promotions seems to be assumed and is occasionally exercised. —ADM.-ADV. COMM. PRAC. (Unwr.)

SARAH LAWRENCE. Faculty member may meet with Advisory Committee on Appointments, or president, or both, before decision that he is not to be reappointed is made. (He may, if he wishes, meet first with only the elected members.) He may name any other persons he would like to have consulted about his work. Before meeting with committee, "he will be provided with an agenda stating the aspects of his work which are to be discussed."—FAC. REG. (*Fac. B-L*)

SWARTHMORE. No official provisions.

VASSAR. Decision not to reappoint may be made only after consultation with department concerned and with Advisory Committee. Any faculty member has right to review by Advisory Committee of reasons given by department for not recommending reappointment.—FAC. REG. (*Ac. Stat.*)

WESLEYAN. No explicit official provisions. In practice, privilege of meeting with president and Advisory Committee is freely granted.—ADM.-ADV. COMM. PRAC. (Unwr.)

6-b. Definition of grounds for dismissal.

COLGATE. Only "cause" is specified, except that "moral turpitude" is included by implication (see Item 6-g).—TRUS. REG. (*Hdbk.*)

HAVERFORD. "Moral turpitude" and "failure to perform academic duties satisfactorily" (including incompetence) are specified. "Disability" of appointee also constitutes formal reason for separation action in spite of continuous tenure; calls for same due process as dismissal.—MGRS. REG. (*Fac. Info.*)

HOBART. "Adequate cause," of which "personal incompetence" is only example specifically mentioned. However, term *dismissal* applies to other situations besides those involving discredit to teacher. Separation under "financial exigency" or "necessary change in educational policy" is also subject to same due process as dismissal (as defined here).—B-L of Trus.

MOUNT HOLYOKE. No grounds specified in formal college documents. Note, however, endorsement of AAUP–AAC *Principles*, which imply that incompetence and moral turpitude are among valid reasons for dismissal.—TRUS.-ADM. POL. (*Hdbk.*)

SARAH LAWRENCE. No official provisions.

SWARTHMORE. Failure or serious shortcomings in carrying out duties ("failure to perform his duties in a manner which measures up to the standard required by the best interests of the institution"). "Grave moral delinquency" also mentioned as cause for dismissal.—MGRS.-FAC. REG. ("Joint Resolution Concerning Faculty Tenure"; also in *Fac. Regs.*)

VASSAR. No complete statement of grounds for dismissal; treason, immorality, and gross neglect of duty recognized as causes.—TRUS.-FAC. REG. (*Ac. Stat.*)

WESLEYAN. To "be deemed to be incompetent, unfaithful or immoral, or otherwise unfit" constitutes grounds for dismissal.—*Charter.*

6-c. Requirement of formal statement of charges, if the teacher requests it, in dismissal proceedings.

COLGATE. Teacher shall be informed in writing before the hearing (if he elects to have hearing) of charges against him.—TRUS. REG. (*Hdbk.*)

HAVERFORD. Formal statement of charges required.—MGRS. REG. (*Fac. Info.*)

HOBART. Statement of cause must be given teacher.—*B-L of Trus.*

MOUNT HOLYOKE. No explicit official provisions. Endorsement of AAUP–AAC *Principles* (TRUS.-ADM. POL. [*Hdbk.*]) implies that written statement of charges must be given if teacher requests it.

SARAH LAWRENCE. No explicit official provisions. Same recourse is assumed as in case of non-reappointment (see Item 6-*a*).—FAC. REG. (By adm. interp. of *Fac. B-L*)

SWARTHMORE. Faculty member has right to formal statement of reasons for "dismissal or demotion" and to same period of notice as required in cases of non-reappointment.—MGRS.-FAC. REG. ("Joint Resolution Concerning Faculty Tenure"; also in *Fac. Regs.*)

VASSAR. Formal statement of charges required if teacher requests it.—TRUS.-FAC. REG. (*Ac. Stat.*)

WESLEYAN. Due notice must be given to accused, and to each trustee, of proposed board action.—*Charter.*

6-d. Guarantee of a hearing, if the teacher requests it, before decision to dismiss is made.

COLGATE. Hearing before committee of three faculty members "designated by the Faculty in consultation with the President of the University and the President of the Board of Trustees." Provisions covering adviser-

142

counsel for accused, stenographic record of hearing, sources of testimony, and report of hearing to trustees.—TRUS. REG. (*Hdbk.*)

HAVERFORD. Hearing before joint meeting of board and faculty committees. Conditions and conduct of hearing follow AAUP–AAC *Principles* in adapted form.—MGRS. REG. (*Fac. Info.*)

HOBART. If teacher denies cause and demands hearing, such a hearing is held before joint trustee-faculty committee consisting of equal number of professors or associate professors and trustees.—B-L *of Trus.*

MOUNT HOLYOKE. No explicit official provisions. Endorsement of AAUP–AAC *Principles* (TRUS.-ADM. POL. [*Hdbk.*]) implies that hearing must be held before every group that passes upon case if teacher requests it, provision being made for adviser-counsel, stenographic record, admission of testimony, etc. Since Advisory Committee on Appointments, Reappointments, and Promotions recommends on matters of dismissal (TRUS.-ADM. REG. [*Hdbk.*]), initial hearing would presumably be held by this group.

SARAH LAWRENCE. No explicit official provisions. Procedure assumed to be same as in case of non-reappointment—that is, meeting of faculty member with Advisory Committee on Appointments, or president, or both (see Item 6-*a*).—FAC. POL. (By interp. of *Fac. B-L*)

SWARTHMORE. No explicit official provisions. AAUP–AAC *Principles* would presumably apply, since they are in general followed as policy on tenure, though not formalized as such.—ADM. POL. (Unwr.; writer's interp.)

VASSAR. Hearing by Advisory Committee if teacher requests it, due consideration being given to any testimony teacher may wish to introduce.—TRUS.-FAC. REG. (*Ac. Stat.*)

WESLEYAN. According to *Charter,* charges alone are sufficient for board to dismiss (see Item 6-*b*). However, trustee *By-Laws* also specify an investigation of charges, without further statement as to what procedure is to be carried out. In cases of pending dismissal for extraordinary cause, such as disloyalty or immorality, joint trustee-faculty committee (three trustees appointed by president of board and two faculty members appointed by Academic Council) is designated to conduct hearing and make recommendation to board.—TRUS.-FAC. REG. (In minutes of both bodies.)

6-e. Guarantee of a further hearing before a higher authority, if the teacher appeals.

COLGATE. No provision for appeal or second hearing.

HAVERFORD. No provision for second hearing. Board committee participates in first hearing, together with faculty committee (see Item 6-*d*).

143

HOBART. Second hearing by board itself is required for dismissal action if joint committee does not recommend dismissal.—*B-L of Trus.*

MOUNT HOLYOKE. No explicit official provisions. AAUP–AAC *Principles* would presumably apply (see Item 6-*d*).

SARAH LAWRENCE. No explicit official provisions. It is assumed that further hearing would be held before second committee if faculty member wished to question recommendation of Advisory Committee on Appointments after initial hearing (see Item 6-*a*).—FAC. REG. (By adm. interp. of unwr. fac. pol.)

SWARTHMORE. No explicit official provisions. AAUP–AAC *Principles* would presumably apply (see Item 6-*d*).

VASSAR. Teacher may appeal from Advisory Committee and have hearing before trustee Committee on Faculty and Studies. Trustees, however, may not act against recommendation of president and Advisory Committee without first affording opportunity for conference.—TRUS.-FAC REG. (*Ac. Stat.*)

WESLEYAN. No official provisions.

6-*f. Action required to make dismissal final.*

COLGATE. Board of trustees makes "final disposition" after receiving report of hearing.—TRUS. REG. (*Hdbk.*) Majority vote of all members of board is necessary to dismiss.—*Charter.*

HAVERFORD. Final decision rests with board.—MGRS. REG. (*Fac. Info.*)

HOBART. Majority vote of trustees necessary if joint trustee-faculty committee recommends dismissal; three-fourths vote of trustees necessary if joint trustee-faculty committee does not recommend dismissal.—*B-L of Trus.*

MOUNT HOLYOKE. No specific provisions. Presumably same procedures apply as for any action of board of trustees.—WRITER'S INTERP.

SARAH LAWRENCE. No specific provisions. Presumably same procedures apply as for any action of board of trustees.—WRITER'S INTERP.

SWARTHMORE. No specific provisions. Presumably same procedures apply as for any action of board of managers.—WRITER'S INTERP.

VASSAR. Affirmative vote of majority of all trustees required.—*Charter* Recommendation of president and Advisory Committee must precede

144

oard action, though trustees are not bound by it.—TRUS.-FAC. REG. (*Ac. tat.*)

WESLEYAN. Two-thirds vote of trustees present and voting is sufcient for dismissal.—*Charter;* also *B-L of Trus.*

-g. *Guarantee of an equitable salary settlement in case of dismissal.*

COLGATE. Salary continues for one year after notification of dismissal, vhether or not teacher is kept on, except in cases involving moral turpitude. –TRUS. REG. (*Hdbk.*)

HAVERFORD. Salary continues for one year after notification of disaissal, except in cases involving moral turpitude.—MGRS. REG. (*Fac. Info.*) ee Item 5-*a* for salary adjustment under other circumstances of separation.

HOBART. No official provisions.

MOUNT HOLYOKE. No explicit provisions. Endorsement of AAUP– ᴧAC *Principles* (TRUS.-ADM. POL. [*Hdbk.*]) implies salary to be continued ne year after notification of dismissal, whether or not teacher is kept on, xcept in cases involving moral turpitude.

SARAH LAWRENCE. No official provisions.

SWARTHMORE. No official provisions.

VASSAR. Salary settlement may not be less than that provided for nder rules for normal resignation (same fraction of annual salary as numer of weeks served is of the thirty-eight weeks in academic year).— RUS. REG. (*Ac. Stat.*)

WESLEYAN. No official provisions.

'rinciple 7: **The right to be governed by a salary policy that is understood, consistent, and determined in the light of consultation with those affected by it.**

-a. *Existence of a published salary scale.*

COLGATE. Salary scale adopted by board lists minimum but not ᴧaximum figures.—TRUS. REG. (*Hdbk.*) Scale published in *Faculty Handook.*

HAVERFORD. Salary scale adopted by board.—MGRS. POL. (*Fac. Info.*) cale published in *Information for Members of the Faculty.*

145

HOBART. Salary scale adopted by board. Not published but available —TRUS. POL. (In trus. minutes.)

MOUNT HOLYOKE. No published salary scale. Board does follow a scale as a matter of policy; median figures for each rank have on occasion been published.—TRUS.-ADM. PRAC. (Unwr.)

SARAH LAWRENCE. No official salary scale (no academic ranks, therefore, usual formal basis for different salary levels is lacking). Note that faculty has much control over both formulation (Item 7-*b*) and administration (Items 3-*b* and 7-*c*) of salary policy.

SWARTHMORE. No official salary scale.—MGRS. PRAC. (Unwr.)

VASSAR. Salary scale adopted by board. Scale must be given to all faculty members, including new members as appointed. Every change in scale must be communicated to all faculty members.—TRUS. REG. (*Ac. Stat.*) Scale published in separate bulletin.

WESLEYAN. Salary scale available, with both minimum and normal maximum figures for each rank.—TRUS. POL. (Pub. in bull.) All full professors reach maximum salary at fifty-eight (ten years before retirement).— TRUS. POL. (Pub. in bull.)

7-b. Faculty participation in the shaping of salary policy.

COLGATE. No official provisions.

HAVERFORD. No explicit official provisions governing formulation of salary policy. In practice, president consults faculty informally on changes in general salary levels.—ADM.-FAC. PRAC. (Unwr.) The two faculty representatives on board participate in board decisions on salary policy but not in setting of individual salaries.—MGRS. PRAC. (Unwr.)

HOBART. Advisory Council discusses all salary questions with president. —ADM.-FAC. PRAC. (Unwr.)

MOUNT HOLYOKE. No specific official provisions; however, joint Conference Committee may discuss salary policy (*B-L of Trus.*, as interp.) and has done so (see Item 16-*a*).

SARAH LAWRENCE. Trustee-faculty Committee on Salaries and Leaves of Absence formulates salary policy.—TRUS.-FAC. PRAC. (Unwr.) Advisory Committee on Appointments represents faculty to president in salary matters.—FAC. REG. (*Fac. B-L*)

SWARTHMORE. No official provisions. No official consultation with any faculty group on salary policy, though issues are discussed by president and faculty informally.—ADM.-FAC. PRAC. (Unwr.)

146

VASSAR. Trustees may not make changes in salary policy, other than upward adjustments, without prior conference with committee designated by faculty.—TRUS. REG. (*Ac. Stat.;* also implied in *Prins.*) Advisory Committee must be consulted by president and trustee Committee on Faculty and Studies concerning annual salary budget. Detailed procedures prescribed.—TRUS. REG. (*Ac. Stat.*)

WESLEYAN. Consultative Finance Committee of faculty (all elected representatives) advises president and board on salary policy in general.— TRUS.-ADM.-FAC. PRAC. (Unwr.)

7-c. Provisions concerning upper salary limits of each rank and conformity to scale.

COLGATE. Overlap of salary ranges between ranks can exist without violation of scale, since only minimum figures are stated. Such overlap does exist.—TRUS.-ADM. PRAC. (Unwr.)

HAVERFORD. Individual salaries within scale set by president and vice-president for board approval. Individual salaries not generally known, but no overlap of salary ranges between ranks exists.—ADM. PRAC. (Unwr.)

HOBART. No written provisions regarding conformity to scale. Scale permits overlap of salary ranges between ranks. Promotions not always accompanied by salary increases.—TRUS.-ADM. POL. AND PRAC. (Unwr.)

MOUNT HOLYOKE. No official provisions regarding conformity to scale. Individual salaries subject to annual determination by board.— TRUS.-ADM. REG. (*Hdbk.;* also in letter of appointment.)

SARAH LAWRENCE. No official salary scale. Advisory Committee on Appointments recommends individual salaries as well as salary policy in general; has systematic criteria and procedure for arriving at judgments. Committee works jointly with president (see Item 3-*a*).—ADM.-FAC. PRAC. (Unwr.)

SWARTHMORE. No official salary scale. Individual salary recommendations generally determined by president in consultation with department head.—ADM. PRAC. (Unwr.)

VASSAR. Individual salaries must conform to scale.—TRUS. REG. (*Ac. Stat.*) Salary ranges of different ranks do not overlap.

WESLEYAN. Board reserves right to make exceptions at its discretion. Overlap of salary ranges between ranks opposed by board as general principle.—TRUS. POL. (Pub. in bull.) Board reserves right to decrease salary below stated amount where obligations of service, for any reason (e.g., personal disability of appointee), have not been met.—TRUS. POL.

147

(Pub. in bull.) Salaries set each year on recommendation of president, who has discretionary power within salary scale and budget.—TRUS.-ADM. PRAC. (Unwr.)

Principle 8: The right to such assistance in matters of personal and family responsibility as the institution is in a position to provide, and the obligation to avail oneself of such help as may forestall one's ever becoming an economic liability, moral or legal, of the institution.

8-a. Privileges and obligations in matters of housing.

COLGATE. Limited housing available; housing matters administered by university administration.—ADM. PRAC. (*Hdbk.*)

HAVERFORD. College-owned faculty housing administered by office of president. Policies and practices governing priority in assignments, tenancy after retirement, tenancy of family after faculty member's death, basis of rental, and other landlord-tenant relationships are set forth in separate administrative document.—ADM. POL. (Pub. in bull.)

HOBART. Limited college-owned faculty housing available; housing matters administered by college administration. Only criterion of priority is date of application.—ADM. PRAC. (Unwr.)

MOUNT HOLYOKE. Priority in occupancy of college-controlled faculty housing based only on order of application. Period of tenancy after retirement explicitly limited. Period of tenancy of family after death of faculty member explicitly limited. Building lots purchasable from college at prices below market value. Building loans available from college at low interest rates.—TRUS.-ADM. POL. (*Hdbk.*) Joint Conference Committee formulates policies for board's adoption.—TRUS.-FAC. PRAC. (*B-L of Trus.;* writer's interp.)

SARAH LAWRENCE. No official provisions. No general college-owned faculty housing.

SWARTHMORE. College-owned housing administered by vice-president according to administration policies. Building a home on college land permitted faculty members according to standard agreement.—MGRS. POL. (Unwr., though building agreement is written and in legal form.)

VASSAR. Official statements cover rights and obligations of tenancy and of building on college land. Housing policies and specific allocations determined by trustees with full consideration given to recommendations of faculty Committee on Faculty Housing.—TRUS. REG. (*Ac. Stat.*)

148

WESLEYAN. College-owned housing administered by college administration.—ADM. PRAC. (Unwr.)

8-b. Optional and required participation in insurance, retirement, and other plans to meet personal risks.[11]

COLGATE. Participation in group term life insurance compulsory for faculty members with dependents who do not carry equivalent protection in other insurance. Amount of policy: $10,000 to $2,000, decreasing as age of policyholder increases.—TRUS. REG. (Hdbk.) Participation in TIAA compulsory after three years, with certain qualifications and exceptions. CREF feature added.—TRUS. REG. (Hdbk. and adm. bulls.)

HAVERFORD. Participation in TIAA compulsory after one year if salary is at least the minimum for assistant professor. CREF feature added.—MGRS. REG. (Fac. Info.)

HOBART. Group life insurance plan available, paid mostly by college: $5,000 maximum policy. College pays premium on first $3,000 and participates in remaining $2,000. Participation in TIAA optional; CREF feature also available.—TRUS.-FAC. REG. (Terms stated in letter of appointment.)

MOUNT HOLYOKE. Optional participation in group life insurance plan; premiums paid by insured.—TRUS. REG. (Hdbk.) Participation in pension plan compulsory after one year, with certain qualifications and exceptions. Faculty member given choice between TIAA (CREF feature also available) and an acceptable plan offered by a commercial insurance company.—TRUS. REG. (Hdbk.)

SARAH LAWRENCE. Group life insurance, at expense of college, begins after one year of service. Amount of policy: $1,000 at first; increases by $100 a year to maximum of $2,000. Participation in TIAA compulsory after two years unless exception is made. CREF feature added.—TRUS. REG. (Pub. in bull.)

SWARTHMORE. Group term life insurance compulsory for members within thirty days after appointment, with certain qualifications and exceptions. College contributes half of premium. Participation in TIAA compulsory after three years, with certain qualifications and exceptions. CREF feature added.—MGRS. REG. (Pub. in bull.)

VASSAR. Group life insurance policy of $1,000 paid for by college. Policy increases in value according to rank, with individual paying difference

[11] The following provisions are made by all eight institutions and are, therefore, omitted from further separate listing: (1) Social security participation is automatic for appointees who originally voted for its adoption and for all subsequently appointed, according to federal law. (2) Blue Cross plan is available at expense of insured; participation is optional.

in premium. Participation compulsory to full amount for which individual is eligible.—TRUS. REG. (*Ac. Stat.*) College pays contribution of all faculty members to Workmen's Compensation Fund. Participation in TIAA compulsory for eligible faculty members over thirty years of age. College meets entire cost. CREF feature added.—TRUS. REG. (*Ac. Stat.*)

WESLEYAN. Optional participation in group life insurance plan, premiums paid by insured.—TRUS. REG. (Pub. in Appendix of *B-L of Ac. Coun.*) Disability insurance (paid for by insured) available through business office, but plan is not sponsored by university.—TRUS. PRAC. (Pub. in Appendix of *B-L of Ac. Coun.*)

8-c. An objectively determined time of retirement.

COLGATE. Compulsory retirement at sixty-eight.—TRUS. REG. (*Hdbk.*)

HAVERFORD. Retirement expected at sixty-five.—MGRS. REG. (*Fac. Info.*) By special action of board, full retirement may be postponed.—MGRS. POL. (Unwr.)

HOBART. Voluntary retirement at sixty-five. Compulsory retirement at seventy. By special trustee action, part-time teaching may be allowed for two years after retirement.—TRUS. POL. (Pub. in bull.)

MOUNT HOLYOKE. Retirement normally at close of college year in which sixty-fifth birthday is reached. May be sixty-eighth by special action of trustees.—TRUS. REG. (*Hdbk.*)

SARAH LAWRENCE. Retirement at close of college year in which sixty-fifth birthday is reached.—TRUS. REG. (Stated in all individual contracts.)

SWARTHMORE. Optional retirement at sixty-five; compulsory retirement at sixty-eight.—MGRS. REG. (Unwr.)

VASSAR. Retirement generally required at sixty-five. Action is at pleasure of trustees, depending on (1) health and efficiency of teacher and (2) welfare of college. Retirement for reasons of health may be required at any time on recommendation of Advisory Committee. (Teacher has right to examination by physician chosen by agreement between himself and college.)—TRUS. REG. (*Ac. Stat.*)

WESLEYAN. Retirement at commencement nearest sixty-eighth birthday unless (1) teacher at own option retires between sixty-five and sixty-eight or (2) trustees request continuance until some time between sixty-eight and seventy.—TRUS. REG. (Pub. in Appendix of *B-L of Ac. Coun.*)

8-d. Miscellaneous other privileges.[12]

COLGATE. Free tuition for sons of faculty members and administrative officers if they are accepted for admission.—TRUS. REG. (*Hdbk.*)

HAVERFORD. Half-rate tuition for children of faculty members admitted to Haverford, Bryn Mawr, or Swarthmore.—MGRS. REG. (By inter-college agreement.)

HOBART. Free tuition for dependents of faculty members of three years' standing (occasionally less than three years in practice; no time stipulation in case of full professors).—TRUS. REG. (In board minutes.)

MOUNT HOLYOKE. Quota of tuition-free enrollments for daughters of residents of community gives priority to families of college faculty. Half-rate tuition for faculty members' children in college nursery school.—TRUS. REG. (*Hdbk.*)

SARAH LAWRENCE. Privilege of borrowing up to $500 from college without interest.—TRUS. POL. (Unwr.) Half-rate tuition for children of faculty members, both for enrollment in college and for enrollment in nursery school operated by college.—TRUS. POL. (Unwr.)

SWARTHMORE. Half-rate tuition for children of faculty members admitted to Swarthmore, Bryn Mawr, or Haverford.—MGRS. REG. (By inter-college agreement.)

VASSAR. Sick leave at discretion of trustees. Salary continued for two months, after which college may begin to deduct cost of substitute.—TRUS. REG. (*Ac. Stat.*) Professor becomes professor emeritus of his subject upon retirement.—TRUS. REG. (*Ac. Stat.*) Salary payments made to immediate family or dependents for four to six months after death in service, number of months depending on length of service.—TRUS. REG. (*Ac. Stat.*)

WESLEYAN. Hospitalization for faculty members and their wives, at stated rates.—TRUS. REG. (Pub. in Appendix of *B-L of Ac. Coun.*) Professor emeritus may continue to use title of his chair.—*B-L of Ac. Coun.* (Q-stat.)

[12] Item 8-*d* is not a complete summary for the eight institutions. Leaves of absence other than sick leave are not mentioned here but are included under Items 11-*a* through 11-*e*. Several colleges in the group belong to the Faculty Children's Tuition Exchange Plan, which is not mentioned under Item 8-*d*.

PART II: RIGHTS AND OBLIGATIONS RELATING TO PERSONAL AND PROFESSIONAL FREEDOM AND GROWTH

Principle 9: The right to encouragement and protection in the activities appropriate to a member of a professional body dedicated to the search for and dissemination of truth, and the obligations associated with this right.

9-a. Guarantees relating to academic freedom in general.

COLGATE. AAUP–AAC *Principles* ("Academic Freedom" section) adopted verbatim.—TRUS. REG. (*Hdbk.*)

HAVERFORD. Formal statement of policy on academic freedom, identical in major particulars with AAUP–AAC *Principles.*—MGRS. REG. (*Fac. Info.*)

HOBART. No formally codified provisions. Statement submitted to Commission on Institutions of Higher Education, Middle States Association of Colleges and Secondary Schools, in March, 1953 (in connection with reevaluation) affirms both "the freedom of the teacher to teach the truth as he sees it" and "the freedom of the teacher as citizen . . . ." Teacher obligated to distinguish political from scholarly functions. College's stand on withholding this freedom from "those who . . . would destroy the fundamental principles of our democracy" is consistent with 1953 statement of Association of American Universities.

MOUNT HOLYOKE. AAUP–AAC *Principles* apply, by formal endorsement and by explicit statement in president's letter of appointment to each faculty member.—TRUS.-ADM. POL. (*Hdbk.*)

SARAH LAWRENCE. Statement of policy issued by trustees relating to functions of an educational institution and freedom necessary for their performance. Specifically excludes political affiliation as factor in judging fitness to teach.—TRUS. POL. (Pub. statement.) Statement consistent with AAUP–AAC *Principles,* though not identical with latter document. Faculty Committee on Academic Freedom has function of advising administration and faculty "individually and collectively, on questions of academic freedom," and of cooperating "with the board, the president, and the faculty in the formulation and execution of policies regarding academic freedom."— FAC. REG. (*Fac. B-L*)

SWARTHMORE. No official provisions.

VASSAR. Formal statement concerning teacher's freedom of instruction and research, and his freedom of utterance on controversial matters.—TRUS.

152

REG. (*Ac. Stat.*) Statement consistent with AAUP–AAC *Principles,* but antedates 1940 AAUP–AAC statement.

Individual teacher assured freedom in conduct of courses, subject to aims of department as a whole.—FAC. REG. (*Ac. Stat.*) Classroom utterances may not be published without teacher's permission.—TRUS. REG. (*Prins.*) Problems involving issues of academic freedom must be the subject of conference between faculty and trustee conference committees in every case (see Item 16-*a*).—TRUS. REG. (*Ac. Stat.*)

WESLEYAN. No official provisions, except as stated in Item 10-*a.*

9-*b. Qualifications and obligations relating to guarantee of academic freedom.*

COLGATE. AAUP–AAC *Principles* ("Academic Freedom" section) adopted verbatim.—TRUS. REG. (*Hdbk.*)

HAVERFORD. AAUP–AAC *Principles* apply in major particulars.— MGRS. REG. (*Fac. Info.*) Policy statement of faculty commends members of faculty for taking active part as citizens "in public movements controversial or otherwise."—FAC. POL. (*Fac. Info.*)

HOBART. No official provisions. See, however, statement made to Middle States Association of Colleges and Secondary Schools (Item 9-*a*).

MOUNT HOLYOKE. AAUP–AAC *Principles* apply.—TRUS.-ADM. POL. (*Hdbk.*)

SARAH LAWRENCE. No specific obligations or limitations, other than stipulation, in trustees' statement, that teachers "meet the test of candor, honesty, and scholarly integrity," and "that there be no indoctrination of students with a political, philosophical, or religious dogma."—TRUS. POL. (Public statement.)

SWARTHMORE. No official provisions.

VASSAR. Formal statement (referred to in Item 9-*a*) names corresponding responsibilities, including attention to college duties, integrity of faculty member's public statements, dignity, accuracy, temperateness, and other ideals traditional in liberal education.—TRUS. REG. (*Ac. Stat.*)

WESLEYAN. No official provisions.

9-*c. Provisions governing outside employment while on appointment at the institution.*

COLGATE. Freedom to engage in outside employment "subject to the adequate performance of his other academic duties . . . . Research for

153

pecuniary return should be based upon an understanding with the authorities of the institution."—TRUS. REG. (*Hdbk.*)

HAVERFORD. Engaging in outside activities, whether for pecuniary return or not, to greater extent than is reasonable, may invalidate faculty member's full-time status (for tenure purposes). If there is any possibility of such excess, president's approval must be obtained.—MGRS. REG. (*Fac. Info.*)

HOBART. No explicit provisions. Faculty members expected to keep administration informed of outside activities and to keep such activities from interfering with college duties.—ADM. POL. (Unwr.)

MOUNT HOLYOKE. No explicit provisions. Endorsement of AAUP–AAC *Principles* (TRUS.-ADM. POL. [*Hdbk.*]) implies that outside activities must not interfere with college duties and that receipt of financial compensation for outside activities must be based on understanding with college authorities. In practice, no limit placed on outside activities. Faculty member consults president as matter of courtesy.—ADM.-FAC. PRAC. (Unwr.)

SARAH LAWRENCE. Unless appointment is part-time, outside employment "which might be detrimental to full service to the College" shall not be undertaken, the administration being the judge.—ADM. POL. (In letter of appointment.)

SWARTHMORE. No official provisions.

VASSAR. Teacher has obligation to see that outside activities do not interfere with college duties.—TRUS. REG. (*Ac. Stat.*) Full-time teacher shall not, without approval of department and president, accept paid employment outside college during academic year.—TRUS. REG. (*Ac. Stat.*)

WESLEYAN. No explicit official provisions. President's permission asked, as matter of courtesy, and freely granted.—ADM.-FAC. PRAC. (Unwr.)

9-*d. Provisions governing absence from campus during academic year.*

COLGATE. Absence must be authorized by dean of faculty.—ADM. REG. (*Hdbk.*)

HAVERFORD. Engaging in outside activities, whether for pecuniary return or not, to greater extent than is reasonable, may invalidate faculty member's full-time status (for tenure purposes). If there is any possibility of such excess, president's approval must be obtained.—MGRS. REG. (*Fac. Info.*)

154

HOBART. Permission of president or provost required for faculty member's absence from college function requiring his presence.

MOUNT HOLYOKE. Permission "should be" obtained from president's office for leaving before commencement.—ADM. REG. (*Hdbk.*)

SARAH LAWRENCE. "Absence from campus" has not quite same meaning as in other colleges of group because of number and variety of part-time appointments made feasible by location of college near New York. —WRITER'S INTERP. Faculty members have contractual obligation to be on campus during days and hours specified in appointment. No official provision covering exceptions.

SWARTHMORE. No official provisions.

VASSAR. Permission of department and president necessary for full-time teacher's protracted absence from campus during academic year.—TRUS. REG. (*Ac. Stat.*)

WESLEYAN. No official provisions.

Principle 10: The right to equal consideration with others regardless of creed in religious or other matters.

10-a. Regulations regarding loyalty oaths.

COLGATE. Faculty members must sign "Oath of Allegiance" as prescribed by New York State law.—ADM. REG. (*Hdbk.*)

HAVERFORD. No loyalty oath required.

HOBART. Faculty members must sign "Oath of Allegiance" as prescribed by New York State law.—ADM. REG. (Unwr.)

MOUNT HOLYOKE. Loyalty oath required as prescribed by Massachusetts law.—ADM. REG. (Unwr.)

SARAH LAWRENCE. Faculty members must sign "Oath of Allegiance" as prescribed by New York State law.—ADM. REG. (Unwr.)

SWARTHMORE. No loyalty oath required.

VASSAR. Faculty members must sign "Oath of Allegiance" as prescribed by New York State law.—ADM. REG. (Unwr.)

WESLEYAN. No loyalty oath required.

155

10-*b*. *Guarantee of religious freedom and equality.*

COLGATE. No official provisions.

HAVERFORD. Only obligation imposed is that "faculty are encouraged to attend collections and meetings and are expected to do so at least occasionally."—ADM. POL. (*Fac. Info.*)

HOBART. No order of trustees may exclude anyone from privileges, benefits, or immunities of college because of his religious beliefs.—*Charter.*

MOUNT HOLYOKE. "No denominational test is imposed in the choice of trustees, officers, or teachers or in the admission of students, nor are any denominational tenets or doctrines taught to students."[13]—TRUS. POL. (Statement voted May 23, 1906.)

SARAH LAWRENCE. No official provisions. Note, however, prohibition of religious indoctrination of students (Item 9-*b*).

SWARTHMORE. No official provisions relating to teachers. Students whose education has been interrupted by reason of their taking the pacifist position are guaranteed same rights as veterans.—FAC. REG. (*Fac. Regs.*)

VASSAR. No official provision.

WESLEYAN. No denominational test may ever be used in selection of teachers.—*Charter.*

Principle 11: **The right to assistance from the institution, through sabbatical leave or other means, in furthering one's development as a professional person, and the obligations associated with receipt of such assistance.**

11-*a*. *Designation of persons who may obtain sabbatical leave.*

COLGATE. No official provisions. No sabbatical leave granted. College helps faculty members with subsidized leave in special cases.—TRUS.-ADM. PRAC. (Unwr.)

HAVERFORD. Sabbatical leave recognized in principle and practice. Time served as instructor not reckoned in determining when such leave has been earned. Terms of sabbatical leave specified in minutes of board (March 19, 1937). Interpretations of these provisions embodied in two re-

---

[13] A. C. Cole, *A Hundred Years of Mount Holyoke College* (New Haven, Conn.: Yale University Press, 1940), p. 249.

ports of faculty committees and entered in faculty minutes. President guided by these in administering board regulations.—MGRS.-ADM. POL. (To be included in revision of *Fac. Info.*)

HOBART. In principle, sabbatical leave may be granted once in seven years.—TRUS. REG. (In trus. minutes.) Actually, no such leave currently granted. Leaves of absence with pay may, however, be granted to senior members of faculty for approved reasons.—TRUS.-ADM. POL. (Unwr.)

MOUNT HOLYOKE. Professorial ranks eligible after six years' service.— TRUS. POL. (*Hdbk.*)

SARAH LAWRENCE. Policy is to grant leave to all faculty members once in seven years. Until recently, backlog of eligibles prevented policy's general application, leaves being granted only to faculty members with longer periods of service.—ADM.-FAC. POL. AND PRAC. (Unwr.) Note, however, other leaves available (Item 11-*e*).

SWARTHMORE. No explicit provisions relating to sabbatical leave. A policy of granting such leave, however, does operate, without respect to rank.—MGRS.-ADM. POL. (Unwr.)

VASSAR. No restriction on eligibility for faculty fellowships (term *sabbatical* not used) after three years' service.—TRUS. REG. (*Ac. Stat.*)

WESLEYAN. Sabbaticals intended primarily for professors. Others may be considered, depending on circumstances.—TRUS. POL. (Pub. in Appendix of *B-L of Ac. Coun.*) In practice, associate professors and, sometimes, assistant professors are given such leaves.—TRUS.-ADM. PRAC. (Unwr.)

11-*b*. Provisions for equitable awarding of sabbatical leave.

COLGATE. No official provisions; no sabbatical leaves.

HAVERFORD. Operates on general principle of one leave in seven years. Faculty member has choice of half year at full salary or full year at half salary. Leave subject to managers-administration action in each case. Exact seven-year interval not necessarily required. There may also be more frequent leaves, without pay (see Item 11-*e*).—MGRS.-ADM. POL. (To be included in revision of *Fac. Info.*)

HOBART. In principle, faculty member may receive half year at full salary or full year at half salary in seven years, provided he applies and circumstances of college permit. Leave subject to board action in each case. —TRUS. REG. (In trus. minutes.) No such leave, however, regularly granted.

MOUNT HOLYOKE. Sabbatical awarded (but not guaranteed) after six years' service upon recommendation of department and president. Salary adjustment on general basis of half salary for full year and up to full salary for half year.—TRUS. POL. (*Hdbk.*)

SARAH LAWRENCE. Policy on leaves formulated by trustee-faculty Committee on Salaries and Leaves of Absence.—TRUS.-FAC. PRAC. (Unwr.) Until backlog of leave entitlements was made up, leave was awarded on basis of length of service without such leave. Individual cases decided by president in consultation with Advisory Committee on Appointments.—ADM. PRAC. (Unwr.) See also other type of leave granted (Item 11-*e*).

SWARTHMORE. No explicit official provisions. Actually, leaves may be awarded much more frequently than once in seven years. They may be as frequent as one semester in three and a half years.—MGRS.-ADM. PRAC. (Unwr.)

VASSAR. One year in seven is "reasonable expectation." Faculty member must have plan acceptable to Committee on Research (elected faculty committee that sets up criteria for awards). Recommendations of Committee on Research affect both granting of leave and award of research grant. Any compensation paid to teacher on leave is treated not as salary but as fellowship grant. Half year at full salary is customary. No salary paid as such.—TRUS. REG. (*Ac. Stat.*)

WESLEYAN. Leaves recommended by president; voted by board.—TRUS.-ADM. PRAC. (Unwr.) Required length of service preceding leave usually six years. One semester with salary is usual arrangement.—TRUS.-ADM.-FAC. POL. (Pub. in Appendix of *B-L of Ac. Coun.*)

11-*c*. *Stated or understood obligations associated with award of sabbatical leave.*

COLGATE. No official provisions; no sabbatical leave.

HAVERFORD. Requirements based on action recorded in board minutes and interpreted in reports of two faculty committees (see Item 11-*a*).—MGRS.-ADM. POL. (To be included in revision of *Fac. Info.*)

HOBART. No official provisions; no sabbatical leave, in strict sense, currently granted (see Item 11-*a*).

MOUNT HOLYOKE. Sabbatical leave granted on understanding that greater part of it is to be spent in study (research, investigation, writing).—TRUS.-ADM. POL. (*Hdbk.*)

SARAH LAWRENCE. No official provisions.

158

SWARTHMORE. No explicit official provisions. "A program of study, research, or writing, calculated to lead to the professional advancement of the individual faculty member, is almost always required . . . ."—ADM. PRAC. (Unwr.; as stated to writer.)

VASSAR. Faculty member expected to return for extended period of service ("ethical" obligation only, though formally stated in *Academic Statute*). Written report of activities engaged in during leave must be submitted to Committee on Research.—FAC. REG. (*Ac. Stat.*)

WESLEYAN. No explicit provisions. It is customary for faculty member to present to president a plan for use of leave.—ADM.-FAC. PRAC. (Unwr.)

11-d. Provisions for travel allowance or grants to attend professional meetings.

COLGATE. Travel allowance in budget for attendance at meetings of professional interest. Funds administered by division director according to policies of division and funds allocated.—ADM. REG. (*Hdbk.*)

HAVERFORD. If faculty member attends meeting of national learned society as officer or for purpose of reading a paper, college will pay round trip.—MGRS. REG. (*Fac. Info.*)

HOBART. Travel allowance administered by provost in consultation with department heads.—ADM. PRAC. (Unwr.)

MOUNT HOLYOKE. Limited travel allowance administered by each department.—ADM.-FAC. PRAC. (Unwr.)

SARAH LAWRENCE. Travel allowance administered by college administration for teachers attending professional meetings.—ADM. PRAC. (Unwr.)

SWARTHMORE. Partial defrayment of travel expenses by college; allowance administered by faculty Committee on Travel Allowance.—ADM. POL. AND PRAC. (Pol. set forth by Committee in memo.)

VASSAR. College will pay travel expenses of faculty members attending professional meetings officially, whether representing college, reading paper, or performing other official functions.—TRUS. REG. (*Ac. Stat.*)

WESLEYAN. Regular funds allocated annually; administered by elected faculty Research Committee.—ADM.-FAC. PRAC. (Unwr.)

11-e. Provisions for other assistance in efforts toward professional growth.[14]

COLGATE. Standing Research Committee dispenses grants from available funds to individual faculty members.—FAC. REG. (Unwr.)

HAVERFORD. Frequent leaves of absence without pay awarded in practice, college making personnel adjustments to facilitate.[15]—MGRS.-ADM. PRAC. (Unwr.)

HOBART. Leaves of absence with pay may be approved by trustees under special circumstances (see Item 11-*a*). Frequent leaves granted without pay.—TRUS.-ADM. PRAC. (Unwr.)

MOUNT HOLYOKE. No official provisions.

SARAH LAWRENCE. One faculty fellowship of $4,000 awarded annually to faculty member who has research project to complete.—TRUS.-FAC. POL. (Pub. in bull.) Each year fellowship has been split between two faculty members, each receiving one term of leave.—FAC.-ADM. PRAC. (Unwr.)
New faculty member may name three advisers to discuss with him, on his own initiative, his teaching methods.—FAC. REG. (*Fac. B-L*)

SWARTHMORE. No official provisions.

VASSAR. Faculty-fellowship system covers both equivalent of sabbatical leave and other major personal undertakings requiring leave or financial help. Other minor leaves granted on individual basis, subject to approval of department and president; salary as determined by trustees. Other funds to aid research administered by faculty committee, subject to approval of trustees. Income-producing publications made possible by such grants become property of college up to amount of grant.—TRUS. REG. (*Ac. Stat.*)

WESLEYAN. Research funds controlled by college administered by elected faculty Research Committee.—TRUS.-ADM.-FAC. PRAC. (Unwr.)

[14] A complete summary of provisions under this heading is not feasible here. Only examples of the provisions existing at each college are listed.
[15] Various additional provisions are to be included in the forthcoming revision of *Information for Members of the Faculty*, to be designated *Information for New Members of the Faculty*.

Principle 12: The obligation to exercise one's professional freedom within the limits of service to the educational enterprise of which one is a member.

12-a. Provisions governing adherence to academic schedule.

COLGATE. Schedule of class meetings must be adhered to, unless dean of faculty authorizes exception.—FAC. REG. (*Hdbk.*)

HAVERFORD. Occasional cancellation of class allowed at teacher's discretion; shifts in hours must be cleared with dean.—ADM. REG. (*Fac. Info.*)

HOBART. Some regulations concerning adherence to schedule exist; not systematically edited or codified as yet.

MOUNT HOLYOKE. Changes in class hours must be reported to registrar.—ADM. REG. (*Hdbk.*)

SARAH LAWRENCE. No official provisions on adherence to schedule. Note, however, reference to contractual obligation to keep certain campus hours (Item 9-*d*).

SWARTHMORE. Formal faculty regulations concerning teacher's obligations in following schedule.—FAC. REG. (*Fac. Regs.*)

VASSAR. No official provisions except as stated in Item 9-*c*.

WESLEYAN. No official provisions.

12-b. Provisions governing maintenance of academic standards and purposes.[16]

COLGATE. Maintenance of academic standards is responsibility of dean of faculty. Official provisions largely concern routine matters in conduct of instruction, examinations, and reporting.—FAC.-ADM. REG. (*Hdbk.*)

HAVERFORD. Faculty considers competence in style and correctness in written composition in evaluating all student work. In principle, total work student does in connection with one course—in class and outside—is limited to nine hours weekly, assuming he carries five full courses.—FAC. POL. (*Fac. Info.*) Basis of grading defined by faculty action.—FAC. POL. (*Fac. Info.*)

[16] A complete summary of provisions under this heading is not feasible here. Only certain examples of the provisions existing at each institution are listed.

161

HOBART. No official provisions.

MOUNT HOLYOKE. Each teacher must relate his distribution of grades to college grading policy and may be asked to justify any deviation. —FAC. REG. (*Hdbk.*) In practice, this rule has not been invoked.

SARAH LAWRENCE. Every instructional activity subject to annual review by faculty Committee on Curricular Problems.—FAC. REG. (By interp. of *Fac. B-L*) Advisory Committee on Appointments reports at least annually to faculty on teaching standards and criteria.—FAC. REG. (*Fac. B-L*) Findings on performance of individual members, however, are not reported to faculty.

Note also the prohibition of religious, philosophical, or political indoctrination of students (Item 9-*b*).

SWARTHMORE. Faculty-legislated norms exist for distribution of student grades in certain types of courses. Grade distributions varying widely from norm are to be brought to instructor's attention.—FAC. REG. (*Fac. Regs.*) No enforcement provided for.

Official regulations exist regarding reports on students' work and standards to be met.—FAC. REG. (*Fac. Regs.*)

VASSAR. Teacher's freedom in conduct of his courses is subject to aims of department as whole.—FAC. REG. (*Ac. Stat.*) See also Item 13-*a*.

WESLEYAN. No official provisions.

Principle 13: The obligation to observe duly the rights and responsibilities of students.[17]

13-*a. The obligation to be as fair as possible in evaluating students' academic work and in determining a student's academic status.*

COLGATE. No official provisions.

HAVERFORD. No official provisions.

HOBART. No official provisions.

MOUNT HOLYOKE. Prescribed process exists for removing student from a course.—FAC. REG. (*Hdbk.*)

SARAH LAWRENCE. Committee on Student Work is responsible for reviewing individual programs and evaluating development of individual

---

[17] Only limited aspects of the faculty member's relationship with students are considered here. Detailed provisions relating to student personnel matters are beyond the scope of this study.

162

,tudents. In determining student's status, student's don (faculty member n charge of her program) has vote.—FAC. REG. (*Fac. B-L*)

SWARTHMORE. Detailed regulations exist for evaluating and report-ng on students' work.—FAC. REG. (*Fac. Regs.*)

VASSAR. Student Records Committee and Committee on the Marking System (which reviews all grades) constitute forces for perspective and equity. Student-faculty Curriculum Committee provides opportunity for tudents to discuss their difficulties.—FAC. REG. (*Ac. Stat.;* writer's interp.)

WESLEYAN. No official provisions.

13-*b. Provisions governing faculty members' responsibilities in han-dling cases of academic dishonesty.*

COLGATE. Students must understand clearly what plagiarism is and >e made aware of possible consequences. All cases of academic dis-1onesty must be reported to Committee on Discipline.—ADM.-FAC. REG. (*Hdbk.*)

HAVERFORD. Honor system administered by Student Council, which :arries full responsibility for penalties, except that expulsion from college s subject to approval of college president.—ADM.-STUD. PRAC. (Stud. *Con-titution*)

HOBART. Cases of academic dishonesty must be reported to dean's >ffice, though minor cases may be handled by department. Serious cases >r repeated offenses must be brought before Academic Board (a faculty-administration body).—FAC. REG. (Unwr.)

MOUNT HOLYOKE. Obligation to clarify what constitutes honorable nethod of work in course rests with teacher. Teacher may deal with a irst and minor offense personally, but all cases of academic dishonesty nust be reported to academic dean's office.—FAC. REG. (*Hdbk.*) Further iction may be taken by other authorities. (Academic dean and Judicial Board of Student Government have responsibilities going beyond those of ndividual teacher.)—FAC.-STUD. REG. (*Hdbk.*)

SARAH LAWRENCE. No specific official provisions, though matters of icademic dishonesty fall within faculty jurisdiction. (Not a problem, be-:ause of the lack of scalar grades and closeness of each don to student's vork. Any case of academic dishonesty would be handled jointly by dean ind student's don.—FAC. POL. (Unwr.)

SWARTHMORE. Academic dishonesty cases to be referred by teacher :o student-faculty committee constituted for purpose.—FAC. REG. (*Fac. Regs.*) In practice this is not generally done; faculty and administrative officers handle most cases. If severe disciplinary action is indicated, case referred by dean to Student Affairs Committee.—ADM.-FAC. PRAC. (Unwr.)

VASSAR. Matters of academic dishonesty fall within jurisdiction of Vassar College Government Association. President may withdraw a case from its jurisdiction; also, no action "in cases involving contractual relations with the college" is legal unless taken by president.—FAC.-STUD. AGREEMENT (Authorized by trus. reg. in *Ac. Stat.*)

WESLEYAN. Honor system administered by student body. Honor System Committee (composed entirely of students) may recommend penalties, including suspension or dismissal, to faculty.—FAC.-STUD. REG. (*Constitution of the College Body*)

13-c. *Provisions governing the giving of help to individual students.*

COLGATE. No official provisions.

HAVERFORD. Functions of faculty advisers stated in document prepared in March, 1953, for Middle States Association of Colleges and Secondary Schools, in connection with accreditation of college.

HOBART. No official provisions.

MOUNT HOLYOKE. No official provisions.

SARAH LAWRENCE. Helping of students, through individual student-don cooperation, is nucleus of academic program rather than accessory to it. Role of don treated in numerous faculty and student documents. Acting as don is one of teacher's specific contractual obligations (as stated in letter of appointment).—WRITER'S INTERP.

SWARTHMORE. No official provisions.

VASSAR. Student advisory system is under joint control of students and faculty. Obligations of both are explicitly stated in *Student Handbook* and other documents.—STUD.-FAC. REG. (*Ac. Stat.*) Tutoring for pay a member of student body is forbidden to faculty members above rank of assistant, and to any assistant in subjects in which he gives examinations.—TRUS. REG. (*Ac. Stat.*)

WESLEYAN. No official provisions.

PART III: RIGHTS AND OBLIGATIONS RELATING TO THE FACULTY MEMBER'S SHARE IN DIRECTING THE EDUCATIONAL ENTERPRISE

Principle 14: The right to work in a departmental or divisional unit that is reasonably free from the arbitrary domination of an individual or a limited group.

14-a. Manner of selection and term of tenure of department[18] chairman (and of division chairman if the latter has major administrative responsibilities).

COLGATE. Department chairmen and division heads appointed.— TRUS.-ADM. PRAC. (Unwr.) Chairman generally appointed for indefinite period.—TRUS.-ADM. REG. (*Hdbk.*)

HAVERFORD. Chairman holds continuous appointment; chairmanship, however, is subject to review at any time by president.—ADM. POL. (Unwr.)

HOBART. Chairman holds continuous appointment.—TRUS.-ADM. PRAC. (Unwr.)

MOUNT HOLYOKE. President must consult all members (instructor and above) of department before recommending appointment to trustees. Appointment is for "specific number of years."—*B-L of Trus.* Department may take secret ballot and make recommendation to president. Appointment is for three-year term and is to be rotated whenever practicable.— TRUS. POL. (As interp. by trus.-fac. Joint Conference Committee and quoted in *Hdbk.*)

SARAH LAWRENCE. No academic departments exist as such. The staffs of the various areas of the curriculum operate as informal departmental units in curriculum planning but have no major administrative significance. Chairman is more group secretary than executive. Chairmanship rotates.—FAC. PRAC. (Unwr.)

SWARTHMORE. Department chairmen and division heads appointed. Rotation not recognized as general principle.—ADM. PRAC. (Unwr.)

VASSAR. Chairmen elected by members of department who have faculty suffrage. Chairman's term two years; he may be re-elected. Only

---

[18] The term *department* as used in this connection denotes any permanent administrative subdivision of the faculty.

165

professors and associate professors eligible, unless no members of those ranks in department.—FAC. REG. (*Ac. Stat.*)

WESLEYAN. Department administered by members of highest rank acting as committee, no one having authority of chairman (in sense of administrative head).—*B-L of Ac. Coun.* (Q-stat.) In practice, members of highest rank serve as chairman in rotation, usually on basis of *primus inter pares.*—FAC. PRAC. (Unwr.)

14-b. Participation of department members in decisions on appointments and promotions.[19]

COLGATE. No official provisions at departmental level. Department chairman and division director consult their colleagues informally, seeking opinions most pertinent to each case.—ADM. PRAC. (Unwr.) See Items 3-*a* and 3-*b* for amplification.

HAVERFORD. No official provisions at departmental level. On less important appointments, informal consultation by president with department chairman and others involved. On more important appointments, *ad hoc* committees are frequently appointed by president.—ADM.-FAC. PRAC. (Unwr.) See Items 3-*a* and 3-*b* for amplification.

HOBART. No official provisions at departmental level. Individuals whose views are especially pertinent are consulted by president and/or Advisory Council.—ADM.-ADV. COUN. PRAC. (Unwr.) See Items 3-*a* and 3-*b* for amplification.

MOUNT HOLYOKE. No explicit official provisions, except in one department (see Item 14-*c*), in which procedure for making nominations affecting appointments and promotions is prescribed by departmental constitution. Other departments follow various unwritten procedures, ranging from formal voting to informal consultation.—WRITER'S INTERP. See Items 3-*a* and 3-*b* for amplification.

SARAH LAWRENCE. No academic departments exist as such. Advisory Committee on Appointments makes recommendations to president on all appointments and increases in salary.—ADM.-FAC. POL. (*Fac. B-L*) President and Advisory Committee consult widely among faculty.—ADM.-FAC. PRAC. (Unwr.) See Items 3-*a* and 3-*b* for amplification.

SWARTHMORE. No official provisions at departmental level. On less important appointments, president and department chairman tend to reach

---

[19] This item is included as an aspect of the faculty member's role in directing the educational enterprise of which he is a member. For consideration of appointment and promotion processes as they affect his *own* case, see Items 3-*a* and 3-*b*.

decisions jointly; on appointments of general faculty concern, president frequently appoints advisory *ad hoc* committee.—ADM.-FAC. PRAC. (Unwr.) See Items 3-*a* and 3-*b* for amplification.

VASSAR. Each member votes in departmental nomination of candidates below himself in rank.—FAC. REG. (*Ac. Stat.*) In smaller departments "vote" usually taken by informal consultation.—FAC. PRAC. (Unwr.) See Items 3-*a* and 3-*b* for amplification.

WESLEYAN. Advisory Committee required to consult with full professors in each department (stated as applying to policy questions in general but construed to apply also specifically to appointments and promotions). If there is no full professor in department, senior officer *may* be consulted.—B-L of Ac. Coun. (Q-stat.) In practice, recommendation of senior department members carries major weight in decision.—ADM.-AC. COUN. PRAC. (Unwr.) See Items 3-*a*, 3-*b*, and 14-*a* for amplification.

14-c. Participation of department members in the direction of other affairs of the department.

COLGATE. Department chairman personally responsible for supervision of departmental affairs, including budget, instruction, and other matters. His authority subject to review by division director and dean of faculty.—ADM. REG. (*Hdbk.*) Actual operation varies among departments, some being run on basis of consensus in almost all important matters and others being run by chairman personally.—FAC.-ADM. PRAC. (Unwr.)

HAVERFORD. Departmental authority and responsibility not explicitly defined. Departments operate as informal groups, policy and action generally being determined by consensus.—FAC. PRAC. (Unwr.)

HOBART. No official provisions.

MOUNT HOLYOKE. No official provisions in documents of college as a whole. Departments traditionally regarded as self-governing units.— ADM.-FAC. PRAC. (Unwr.) Largest department (English) operates on basis of departmental constitution, which limits powers of chairman to those that seem administratively necessary and spreads authority and responsibility by stipulating use of committees with explicitly stated powers. Other departments work out sharing of authority in less formal manner.

SARAH LAWRENCE. No academic departments exist as such.

SWARTHMORE. No official provisions relating to sharing of departmental authority. Most departments said to operate on basis of consensus. —FAC. PRAC. (Unwr.) Note also divisional meetings (Item 15-*c*).

VASSAR. Any member of department may make suggestions, introduce motions, or participate in discussions. Any member may consult president or Advisory Committee on matters affecting conduct of his department. Matters of concern to department as a whole are to be presented at departmental meetings.—FAC. REG. (*Ac. Stat.*)

WESLEYAN. Matters of departmental administration "should be" subject of conference among all officers of instruction in department, regardless of rank.—*B-L of Ac. Coun.* (Q-stat.) All officers of equal rank have equal rights and privileges in conduct of affairs of their departments.— *B-L of Ac. Coun.* (Q-stat.) Note that this provision is not identical with preceding one.

Annual departmental report to trustees to be prepared by chairman, incorporating partial reports by each individual officer of instruction.—*B-L of Ac. Coun.* (Q-stat.)

14-d. *Provisions designed to assure equitable distribution of the teaching load.*

COLGATE. No faculty member required to have more than half his teaching assignment devoted to core program unless he so wishes.—ADM.-FAC. REG. (*Hdbk.*) Teaching loads assigned by department chairmen, subject to review by division director and dean of faculty.—ADM. REG. (*Hdbk.*)

HAVERFORD. No official provisions.

HOBART. No official provisions.

MOUNT HOLYOKE. No official provisions.

SARAH LAWRENCE. No academic departments exist as such. Teaching load based on fraction of full-time appointment for which faculty member's contract is drawn. Instructional and advisory loads assigned without regard to seniority. Some modification may be made in assignment because of assumption of other responsibilities. Advisory Committee on Appointments advises president on assignment of teaching load.—FAC. REG. (*Fac. B-L*)

SWARTHMORE. No official provisions.

VASSAR. In allocation of teaching loads, all pertinent factors must be considered, not just number of teaching hours. Pertinent factors explicitly stated.—FAC. REG. (*Ac. Stat.*)

WESLEYAN. "It is desirable that there should not be marked inequalities between officers of instruction in the amount of class work under their charge." Nine to twelve hours per week considered desirable teach-

168

ing load; modifications may be made because of health, research activities, other duties, etc.—*B-L of Ac. Coun.* (Q-stat.)

Principle 15: The right and the obligation to play a responsible role in the over-all functions appropriate to a college faculty.

15-a. Definition of the responsibility and the authority of the faculty as a whole.

COLGATE. Authority and responsibility of faculty, subject to board approval, extend to courses of study, rules and methods for conduct of educational program, and student discipline. President responsible for carrying out measures agreed on by faculty concerning matters committed to faculty by board. Elsewhere in same document, however, president is given "general oversight and direction of the University instruction and discipline." Responsibilities of president and faculty further stated at some length.—*B-L of Trus.*

HAVERFORD. No statutory definition of authority and responsibility of faculty. Document setting forth functions of faculty was prepared in March, 1953, for Middle States Association of Colleges and Secondary Schools, in connection with accreditation of college.

HOBART. "The work in instruction in the Colleges shall be committed to the faculties under the direction of the President."—*B-L of Trus.*

MOUNT HOLYOKE. Powers and duties of faculty, including responsibility for educational policy and program and for student life program, are set forth at length. All are "subject to the reserve power of control of the Board . . . ." Two major qualifications: (1) Any matter of "major issue in the educational policy or social functioning of the College" (in judgment of president) is subject to approval of president and board. (2) "Changes of a major nature in the academic or social functioning of the College shall require consultation between Faculty and Trustees, unless there be agreement between the two bodies."—*B-L of Trus.* See also provisions for trustee-faculty conference (Item 16-*a*).

SARAH LAWRENCE. No written statement of faculty authority and responsibility. *Faculty By-Laws,* however, prescribe policies and procedures in certain areas of administration. Board's acceptance of *Faculty By-Laws* implies delegation of certain administrative matters (including appointments, promotions, and budget) to faculty.—WRITER'S INTERP.

SWARTHMORE. No provisions in current codified legislation.

VASSAR. Authority and responsibility of faculty explicitly stated. "The Faculty shall in general determine and shall direct educational policy."

169

Specific faculty jurisdictions named. Certain matters, including important educational changes or changes requiring considerable financial adjustment, must be referred to trustee-faculty conference.—TRUS. REG. (*Prins.*)

WESLEYAN. "The administration of the University shall be vested in the Faculty . . . provided that every act of executive administration shall have the concurrence of the President." Specific powers and duties of faculty as a whole and of heads of academic departments and divisions also stated.—*B-L of Trus.*

15-b. Definition of faculty membership.[20]

COLGATE. President and those whose duties are primarily instructional or "in the direct supervision of" instruction (professors, associate professors, assistant professors, instructors) have faculty membership.—*B-L of Trus.* By interpretation, members of professional library staff also included.

HAVERFORD. No official definition. Attendance at faculty meetings expected of all ranks (instructor and above), of designated members of administration, and of visiting professors and lecturers.—ADM. REG. (*Fac. Info.*)

HOBART. No official definition. Both *Charter* and trustee *By-Laws* imply that instructors are faculty members.—WRITER'S INTERP.

MOUNT HOLYOKE. President, academic dean, dean of residence, registrar, director of admissions, librarian, resident physicians, professors, associate professors, assistant professors, instructors, and departmental assistants are faculty members.—*B-L of Trus.* Others may be given faculty membership by special trustee action. Nine accorded such membership at present, including four of professional library staff.

SARAH LAWRENCE. "General faculty" comprises all teachers, all members of academic administration, and all members of business administration.—FAC. REG. (*Fac. B-L*) "Teaching faculty," as distinguished from "general faculty," not officially defined. Is understood to include librarian but to exclude those who are primarily administrative officers.—FAC. PRAC. (Unwr.)

SWARTHMORE. Professors, associate professors, assistant professors, full-time instructors, and designated administrative officers are faculty members.—MGRS.-FAC. REG. (In board minutes.)

VASSAR. "All members of departments of instruction" are faculty mem-

---

[20] Note that faculty membership does not necessarily carry the right to vote on all matters entrusted to the faculty (Item 15-c).

170

bers.—FAC. REG. (*Ac. Stat.*) Lecturers, assistants, consultants, and other special appointees included.

WESLEYAN. President, professors, associate professors, assistant professors, instructors, and other officers as determined by vote of board are faculty members.—*B-L of Trus.* "Other officers" having faculty membership, either by vote of board or by virtue of holding separate appointment as professor, include dean of faculty, head librarian, and vice-president in charge of business affairs.

15-c. Definition of voting rights.

COLGATE. Voting rights extended to all faculty members except (1) those serving on part-time or temporary appointment and (2) instructors with less than two years' service. Following administrative officers have voting rights: deans, associate deans, registrar, librarian, secretary of university, treasurer of university, university chaplain, university physician, and others as designated "from time to time" by president with board approval.—*B-L of Trus.*

HAVERFORD. No official provisions governing franchise. Accepted procedure is to reach decisions by consensus.—FAC. POL. AND PRAC. (Unwr.)

HOBART. Officially, instructors with less than one year's service do not have voting rights.—FAC. REG. (In fac. minutes.) Actually, all members vote except on crucial issues and in electing committees, when official rule is likely to be invoked.—FAC. PRAC. (Unwr.)

MOUNT HOLYOKE. Voting rights extended to president; academic dean; dean of residence; and to officers of instruction (professors, associate professors, assistant professors, lecturers, and instructors), in subjects counting toward a degree, after they have completed one year of full-time service or its equivalent at Mount Holyoke.—*B-L of Trus.*

SARAH LAWRENCE. No official provisions governing franchise. Voting rights presumed to be conferred by membership in faculty (see Item 15-*b*).—FAC. PRAC. (Unwr.)

SWARTHMORE. No official provisions governing franchise. Voting rights presumed to be conferred by membership in faculty (see Item 15-*b*). —FAC. PRAC. (Unwr.)

VASSAR. Voting rights in matters of educational policy extended to full-time teachers (instructor and above) after one year's service; to half-time (or more) teachers (instructor and above) after two years' service; to president, dean, assistant dean, and (by vote of faculty) assistant to president.—FAC. REG. (*Ac. Stat.*) On matters other than educational policy,

171

suffrage is broader.—FAC. REG. (*Ac. Stat.*) Most important questions, however, are interpreted as involving educational policy. Rule stated above excludes professional library staff, warden, chaplain, and director of admissions from voting on educational matters. It does not, however, apply to individuals who had voting rights before it was passed.—ADM.-FAC. PRAC. (By interp. of *Ac. Stat.*)

WESLEYAN. No official provisions. All four instructional ranks assumed to have right to vote.—FAC. PRAC. (Unwr.)

15-d. Frequency of faculty meetings.

COLGATE. One meeting per month.—ADM.-FAC. PRAC. (*Hdbk.*)

HAVERFORD. One meeting per month.—ADM.-FAC. PRAC. (*Fac. Info.*)

HOBART. One meeting per month.—ADM.-FAC. PRAC. (Unwr.)

MOUNT HOLYOKE. One meeting per month.—*B-L of Trus.* Special meetings called by president on own initiative or on request of Board of Advisers or of any twenty faculty members.—ADM.-FAC. REG. (*Hdbk.*)

SARAH LAWRENCE. One meeting per week unless no agenda, in which case meeting is skipped.—FAC. PRAC. (Unwr.)

SWARTHMORE. No stated meetings. Four to five held per year.— ADM.-FAC. PRAC. (Unwr.) Each academic division has luncheon meeting every two weeks.—FAC. PRAC. (Unwr.)

VASSAR. No official requirement as to frequency of meetings. Held on call of president or on petition of ten faculty members.—FAC. REG. (*Ac. Stat.*) In practice, meetings held at least once a month (oftener if necessary).— ADM.-FAC. PRAC. (Unwr.)

WESLEYAN. No official provisions concerning general faculty meetings. Approximately one per month. Divisional meetings at least once a semester (oftener at direction of faculty, at call of division chairman, or at request of three members).—*B-L of Ac. Coun.* (Q-stat.)

15-e. Guaranteed rights of participation in faculty deliberations.

COLGATE. Any faculty member may make proposals on educational policy at regular faculty meetings, without submitting them first to faculty-administration Committee on Educational Policy.—FAC. REG. (*Hdbk.*) Instructors, assistants, and administrative officers on at least a one-year appointment may take part in deliberations (but not vote).—*B-L of Trus.*

HAVERFORD. No official provisions.

172

HOBART. No official provisions.

MOUNT HOLYOKE. Right of discussion at faculty meetings explicitly assured to all members.—FAC. REG. (*Hdbk.*)

SARAH LAWRENCE. No official provisions.

SWARTHMORE. No official provisions.

VASSAR. Matters of concern to faculty as a whole shall be presented at faculty meetings.—FAC. REG. (*Ac. Stat.*)

WESLEYAN. No official provisions.

15-f. Provision for fair representation on faculty policy-making, administrative, and judicial committees.

COLGATE. Following are important examples of wholly or partly elected faculty bodies: (1) faculty-administration Committee on Educational Policy (nine members elected from faculty at large, others ex officio); (2) certain key standing committees (all elected except for certain ex officio administrative members). Members of other standing committees partly ex officio and partly appointed by president with approval of faculty-administration Committee on Educational Policy. Two committees concerned with student affairs and discipline also may have elected student members. —FAC. REG. (By adoption of report of an *ad hoc* committee, 1951.)

HAVERFORD. Committees in general appointed by president with advice of Academic Council.—ADM.-FAC. PRAC. (*Fac. Info.*)

HOBART. Following are important examples of wholly or partly elected faculty bodies: (1) President's Advisory Council (three professors elected by faculty, plus four administrative officers ex officio); (2) Conference Committee (three elected faculty members); (3) Educational Policy Committee (eight faculty members elected by academic divisions).—ADM.-FAC. REG. (Unwr.)

MOUNT HOLYOKE. Following are important examples of wholly or partly elected faculty bodies: (1) Advisory Committee on Appointments, Reappointments, and Promotions (all elected); (2) Conference Committee (all elected); (3) Committee to Appoint Committees (all elected); (4) Board of Advisers (all elected). Most standing committees partly or wholly elected, according to procedures prescribed in faculty legislation.— FAC. REG. (*Hdbk.*)

SARAH LAWRENCE. All committees of faculty elected. Nominating Committee (itself an elected group) prepares slates for other committees;

173

other nominations may be made from floor.—FAC. REG. (*Fac. B-L*) Faculty-trustee and faculty-student committees operate in certain areas; faculty members of these committees usually elected.—FAC. POL. (*Fac. B-L;* writer's interp.)

SWARTHMORE. No standing elected committees. No formal provisions relating to composition or function of committees. President consults informally on committee appointments. Administration-faculty custom is for president to give faculty (or faculty division concerned) option of election or presidential appointment of each *ad hoc* committee to be constituted; usual outcome is appointed committee.—ADM.-FAC. POL. AND PRAC. (Unwr.)

VASSAR. Following are important examples of wholly or partly elected faculty bodies: (1) Advisory Committee (all elected); (2) Conference Committee (all elected); (3) Committee on Committees (largely elected); (4) Committee on Curriculum (largely elected). Numerous other committees partly or wholly elected. Manner of constituting each committee formally prescribed.—FAC. REG. (*Ac. Stat.*)

WESLEYAN. Following are important examples of wholly or partly elected faculty bodies: (1) Advisory Committee (elected by Academic Council, not faculty at large—see Item 15-g; president and dean of faculty are members ex officio).—*B-L of Ac. Coun.* (Q-stat.) (2) Policy Committee (Advisory Committee plus elected officers of junior faculty). (3) Consultative Finance Committee (elected by full faculty). Most other committees nominated by Nominating Committee (president and three elected division chairmen) and elected by full faculty.—ADM.-FAC. PRAC. (Unwr.)

15-g. *Restrictions and qualifications affecting individual eligibility for membership in faculty policy-making, administrative, and judicial bodies.*

COLGATE. No official restrictions or qualifications.

HAVERFORD. No official restrictions or qualifications.

HOBART. Elected members of Advisory Council are full professors.—FAC. PRAC. (Unwr.; Q-stat.) Elected members of Conference Committee must be full professors.—TRUS. POL. (Unwr.)

MOUNT HOLYOKE. Advisory Committee membership restricted to professors and associate professors who are on "teaching faculty" (as distinguished from administrative officers having faculty status) and have had three years' service.—FAC. REG. (*Hdbk.,* as interp. in prac.) No other official restrictions or qualifications except that on certain committees a member may not serve consecutive terms.—FAC. REG. (*Hdbk.*)

174

SARAH LAWRENCE. Limit of continuous membership on any one committee three years. Number of memberships one person may hold at one time limited to one for certain committees. Also, certain committee memberships must be held by members of "teaching faculty" (as distinguished from "general faculty").—FAC. REG. (*Fac. B-L*)

SWARTHMORE. No official provisions. Committees generally appointed by president (see Item 15-*f*).

VASSAR. Committee membership limited to those who have voting rights. Membership on certain committees restricted on basis of rank—e.g., members of Advisory Committee must be assistant professors, associate professors, or professors; members of Research Committee must be associate professors or professors. Number of committees a person may be on is limited according to specific schedule.—FAC. REG. (*Ac. Stat.*)

WESLEYAN. Only president, full professors, and others who may be appointed to it by trustees may serve on Academic Council.—*B-L of Trus.* Only full professors, plus president and dean of faculty, may serve on Advisory Committee, since it is a committee of Academic Council and not of general faculty.—*B-L of Trus.* (Writer's interp.)

15-*h. Provision for direct access by faculty members to faculty policy-making, administrative, and judicial committees.*

COLGATE. No official provisions.

HAVERFORD. No official provisions.

HOBART. No official provisions.

MOUNT HOLYOKE. Any six faculty members may cause Board of Advisers to meet and may name chairman of meeting. Said six members have right of attendance and discussion.—ADM.-FAC. REG. (*Hdbk.*)

SARAH LAWRENCE. Any faculty group may meet with elected members of Advisory Committee on Appointments. Any faculty member has right to hearing by Advisory Committee at any time.—FAC. REG. (*Fac. B-L*)

SWARTHMORE. No official provisions.

VASSAR. Any faculty member has right to make complaint formally and in writing to president, department, or Advisory Committee. Any faculty member may consult Advisory Committee on matters affecting conduct of his department. Any faculty member may consult informally any Advisory Committee member without necessarily bringing problem to Advisory Committee for formal action.—FAC. REG. (*Ac. Stat.*)

175

WESLEYAN. Faculty member's privilege of a hearing before Advisory Committee freely granted, though no official provision to that effect exists. —ADM.-FAC. PRAC. (Unwr.) Junior faculty members of Policy Committee act as channel of access to Advisory Committee for junior faculty.—FAC. POL. (Unwr.)

Principle 16: The right to a direct means of communication with the governing board of the institution.

16-a. Provisions for faculty conference with, or representation on, the governing board.

COLGATE. Official faculty-trustee communication is through president. —B-L of Trus. Joint trustee-faculty committees operate in certain specific areas, such as (1) religious life of students, (2) library, and (3) business studies.—TRUS.-ADM. PRAC. (Unwr.)

HAVERFORD. Two elected faculty members sit on board. They are not part of board by any statutory enactment but function as voting members and are designated in college catalog as "Faculty Representatives on Board of Managers."—MGRS.-FAC. PRAC. Faculty committees (*ad hoc*) advise board in particular areas (e.g., housing, tenure, and pensions) on request of either body.—MGRS.-ADM.-FAC. PRAC. (Unwr.)

HOBART. Faculty members, other than president, are ineligible for membership on board of trustees.—*Charter.* Conference Committee of faculty (elected) meets at least annually with corresponding committee of board as Joint Conference Committee.—TRUS-FAC. PRAC. (In minutes of both bodies.) Any faculty member is understood to be entitled to consult with faculty Conference Committee.—ADM.-FAC. PRAC. (Unwr.)[21]
Trustee *By-Laws* call for establishment of "Visiting Committees" by board, at least ten areas being designated for committee cognizance.— B-L of Trus. Trustee committees now function in areas of admissions, athletics, and buildings and grounds.

MOUNT HOLYOKE. Conference Committee of trustees meets with elected Conference Committee of faculty as Joint Conference Committee.— B-L of Trus. (Also in Hdbk.) Conference Committee of faculty must take up any matter faculty instructs it to take up with board.—FAC. REG. (Hdbk.) Joint Conference Committee must meet once a year (actually meets two or three times). Any question affecting general welfare of college must be subject of trustee-faculty conference. Action by Joint Conference Committee is not binding until ratified by board of trustees.—B-L of Trus. Except for Joint Conference Committee, only official channel of communi-

[21] No formal understanding exists by which the faculty Conference Committee is answerable to the faculty. One view held is that faculty members of the Committee are free agents, not to be instructed in their role.

176

cation between trustees and faculty is through president.—*B-L of Trus.*
Vice-president and academic dean, however, attend board meetings.—
TRUS. PRAC. (In trus. minutes.)

SARAH LAWRENCE. Teaching faculty nominates one of twenty-two
members elected by board of trustees. Official trustee-faculty communication
is through president. Faculty, however, has right of representation
before board—trustee *By-Laws* guarantee "same right of faculty representation
before the Committee [Executive Committee of the trustees] as before
the Board of Trustees."—*B-L of Trus.* Joint trustee-faculty committees
operate in certain policy-making areas, including those of salary, leaves,
and scholarships.—TRUS.-FAC. POL. (*Fac. B-L*)

SWARTHMORE. Consultation required between board Committee on
Instruction and Libraries and "the appropriate officers" of college on "all
matters pertaining to instruction not delegated by the Board to the
Faculty or the President of the College."—*B-L of the Corp.* No other
regular official channel of communication exists (except, of course, the
president). Board-faculty *ad hoc* committees, however, have operated in
numerous areas, including (1) relations with alumni, (2) determining
future size of college, (3) public relations, (4) selection of president, (5)
academic freedom, (6) honorary degrees, and (7) interesting students in
public service activities of Society of Friends.—MGRS.-ADM.-FAC. PRAC.
(Unwr.)

VASSAR. Principle of conference between faculty and trustees explicitly
recognized by board. Conference Committee of faculty (elected)
meets regularly with similar committee of board.—TRUS. REG. (*Prins.;*
also in *Ac. Stat.*) Other trustee-faculty conference committees have specific
areas of jurisdiction, and subjects with which they are to deal are prescribed
by statute. Neither board nor faculty may act on certain matters
without first referring them to conference through established trustee-faculty
channels.—TRUS. REG. (Partly in *Prins.;* partly in *Ac. Stat.*)

WESLEYAN. System of informal conferences between trustees (chiefly,
trustee Committee on Faculty and Curriculum) and faculty members exists.
Meetings annually or semiannually and on special occasions. Trustee-faculty
administrative and advisory committees operate in certain areas.—
TRUS.-FAC. PRAC. (Unwr.) Academic Council empowered to appoint from
itself a committee to meet with trustee Committee on Faculty and Curriculum
in advance of stated meeting of board.—*B-L of Trus.* Advisory
Committee designated by Academic Council to perform this conference
function.—*B-L of Ac. Coun.* (Q-stat.) Individual faculty members may be
encouraged to take certain matters to appropriate trustee committee.—
ADM. PRAC. (Unwr.)

16-b. *Provisions for faculty participation in the choice of principal officers of the institution.*

COLGATE. No explicit official provisions. Usually, faculty opinion not formally sought in selection of president, though faculty committee was consulted in most recent instance, on faculty initiative.

HAVERFORD. No explicit official provisions. Note, however, faculty representation on board (Item 16-a). In most recent instance of selecting president, two faculty members were elected by faculty to advise board. These two members functioned in effect as members of selection committee. —MGRS.-FAC. PRAC. (Unwr.)

HOBART. No explicit official provisions. In most recent selection of president, elected faculty committee proposed criteria and specific names to board. Faculty not actually represented on selection committee of board.— TRUS.-FAC. PRAC. (Unwr.) Advisory Council advises president on appointment of dean.—ADM.-FAC. PRAC. (Unwr.) President presents nomination to board.—*B-L of Trus.*

MOUNT HOLYOKE. No explicit official provisions. In most recent selection of president, trustees received advice of committee representing faculty. Recommendation was not followed. In most recent selection of academic dean, recommendation of faculty committee was followed.

SARAH LAWRENCE. Faculty Planning Committee (elected) advises trustees on long-range matters, including, in most recent instance, selection of president.—TRUS.-FAC. PRAC. (Unwr.) In most recent selection of dean, president made recommendation to board; faculty participated in selection informally, and also through Advisory Committee on Appointments.— ADM.-FAC. PRAC. (Application of *Fac. B-L*)

SWARTHMORE. No explicit official provisions. In most recent selection of president, *ad hoc* committee of managers and elected representatives of faculty and alumni association was designated to make nomination.— MGRS.-FAC. PRAC. (Unwr.) *Ad hoc* committee of managers, alumni, and faculty members (appointed) nominates deans and vice-president.—MGRS.- ADM.-FAC. PRAC. (Unwr.)

VASSAR. No explicit official provisions for faculty participation in selection of president, except that "conference" provision (see Item 15-a) might be construed to include this matter. In most recent instance, elected faculty committee advised board on selection.—TRUS.-FAC. PRAC. (Unwr.) Faculty committee of five elected to confer with president on nomination of dean. Approval of president and majority of committee necessary for nomination.—TRUS.-FAC. REG. (*Ac. Stat.*)

178

WESLEYAN. No explicit official provisions for faculty participation in selection of president. Informal consultation by trustees, however, is usual.—TRUS. PRAC. (Unwr.) Deans appointed annually by board on nomination of president, after consultative secret ballot of faculty.—*B-L of Ac. Coun.* (Q-stat.)

INDEX

181